Flyers

Peter Brine

ISBN   978-1-913375-07-2

Published by Glenfield Books

info@glenfieldbooks.co.uk

To Hannah

who has inspired so many to sing.

Flyers

Chapter 1: Robert's Epitaph

'May I sit here, please, Mrs Winston?'

Until that moment it had been her usual Sunday routine – breakfast, feed the cat, go to church and then on the bus to visit Robert. But suddenly this was no longer the usual routine. A chill imposed itself on what had been so far a pleasant August afternoon. She looked around and saw several people who would hear her if she screamed.

'I'm sorry, I didn't mean to startle you.'

She thought she recognised the speaker: if she was right he had been there on one or two previous Sundays but they had never spoken before and she had no idea how he knew her name. She drew her coat protectively round herself.

The voice was also surprising. He was a fairly – dapper was the word Robert would have used – middle aged man but the voice was smooth and elegant. And was there a slight accent? She noticed that his clothes were good quality and not old. He wore glasses which gave him a dignified look.

'I'm sorry, do I know you?' she asked. She studied his polished shoes and neatly creased trousers. And he wore a tie. He could be as old as sixty, clean shaven and with his hair trimmed and parted. What Robert would have called well-turned out. According to Robert, the younger generation never bothered to look even tidy, never mind well-dressed. And she caught the scent of a pleasant cologne. She'd never managed to persuade Robert that cologne was OK for a man.

'I don't think so.' He didn't actually look threatening and he didn't sound official.

'So how do you know my name?' She'd heard about stalkers. He didn't look like a stalker, but then she didn't know what a stalker looked like. He looked more like a solicitor, or at least what a solicitor on TV looked like. She'd never met one in real life as far as she knew. He could be a con-man or a mugger.

He sat down on the bench without invitation.

'Oh, elementary, Mrs Winston,' he said, with a gentle smile, 'You're wearing a wedding ring and you regularly put flowers on the grave of Robert Winston so I assumed he was your husband.'

He was right about that. She did regularly visit her beloved Robert's grave. Robert who had died so tragically on New Year's Eve in 2012, just hours before his fiftieth birthday. Robert who had been so looking forward to the family party planned for him. So what did this stranger want with her? She paused and thought for a moment, 'Did you know Robert?'

'I'm afraid not. I'd better explain. It's really quite simple. I come here regularly to visit my late wife, Sylvia. I've often seen you and I thought you might like to join me for a cup of tea? After you've finished here, that is.'

Good Lord, he's trying to chat me up. So soon after Robert left me. I'm fifty two years old and some stranger is chatting me up. She wasn't sure how to respond. In one way she was flattered but she really didn't want to get involved with a man, and certainly not one who tried to hit on her in a cemetery. However, she smoothed her skirt and was pleased she had put her best coat on to visit Robert.

'I wouldn't have mentioned it but I realised we must live close together because I saw you in Brunswick Street newsagents on Tuesday and today I noticed you get off the bus and I thought, well, if we both come here on a Sunday, why couldn't I offer you a lift in my car.'

She tried to remember if she'd been in the newsagents on Tuesday and had she seen him. 'I'm sorry but I don't think that would be appropriate – why I don't even know your name.'

'Well that's easily put right, it's Mr Rossini, Valentino Rossini.'

So that explained the accent and rather formal way of speaking. And was that it? He just wanted to offer her a lift. He could be the Mafia though she couldn't think why they would be interested in her. She was just being silly, letting her imagination run away with her.

'And I promise you I have no ulterior motive. I simply offered the cup of tea because, well, I always have a cup of tea in the cafe just outside the cemetery gates before I drive home.'

'I'm sorry, Mr Rossini, it's a very kind offer, but, with my husband so recently gone....'

'The memorial says he died two and a half years ago – but anyway – it was only an offer of a lift. If your husband was still here would he have not wanted you to avoid the bus journeys?'

'Well...'

'And if you are worried about your safety, do you have a mobile phone?'

"Yes....?'

'Then you can take a picture of me and send it to your children ... and of my car and its number plate. Then if you did disappear, the police would soon know where to look.' This seemed a reasonable suggestion.

'I see.' It certainly would be much easier to have a regular lift on a Sunday. And if he was really visiting his wife's grave. She liked his quiet persistence and gentle charm. She studied him for a moment. If anything, he looked slightly more apprehensive than she was feeling.

'Perhaps I could at least accept your kind invitation to a cup of tea.' Probably not a good idea to mention that her phone didn't take pictures and she had no children. 'Then I'll think about the lift.'

He was certainly very tactful as his next sentence confirmed, 'And if you don't want me to know where you live, I can drop you at the end of the road, or near the shops or where-ever is convenient. I understand that you can't be too careful nowadays.'

'That's very considerate of you, Mr Rossini, but I haven't said....'

'Please, call me Valentino – my friends call me Val.'

'I think I prefer Mr Rossini, if you don't mind.' She realised she probably sounded rather like the school teacher she had been before her widowhood. It was also becoming apparent to her that she had lost the ability to talk naturally to strangers. And she had fewer and fewer opportunities to talk to her friends who had rallied round immediately after the accident but who had begun to visit less and less frequently in the two years following it. Perhaps it would do her good to talk to someone.

'As you wish' He stood up. 'Ready?'

'As I'll ever be,' She gathered up her bags in which she'd brought flowers, trimming scissors and the other bits and pieces she normally took to maintain Robert's grave. She began to think that she may have misjudged this stranger – Mr Rossini – Val - and that he had been quite courageous in approaching her. And if he really had lost his wife he might have some idea of what she had been through.

As they walked towards the cemetery gates she asked about his wife. 'How long have you been a widower?'

Almost as long as you, two years next month.' He paused. 'Ovarian cancer.'

'I'm sorry.'

'Not easy. And Robert? How did you lose Robert?'

She could still barely speak about it. 'It was a road accident. He was on his bike coming back from his sister's and a lorry caught him as it went past. The police said he died instantly. I hope that's true.'

They walked on in silence until Mr Rossini stopped and said, 'This is Sylvia's grave.' It was obviously well tended and there were fresh flowers on it. He paused and she waited with him. After a few minutes of silence, he was ready to move on. They continued out of the cemetery and almost immediately he led her into the tea shop. It was a little like her, she thought, old-fashioned and set in its ways. It was not run down, but its best days were certainly behind it. Shabby chic but without the chic, she thought.

'Hello Mr Rossini,' said the girl behind the counter, 'Your usual?'

'Yes please, Tina.'

'And your friend?'

He turned to her, 'I usually have a cup of tea and a slice of their home made cake. Can I tempt you to the same?'

'I'll get my own, thank you.' He looked a little hurt, and she realised she was being rather abrupt and discourteous. ' Sorry, Mr Rossini. I'm not meaning to be rude but I've been independent for over two years now, I'm used to managing for myself.' Oh what the hell,' Yes please, tea and a slice of that walnut cake would be lovely.'

She saw him relax slightly.

He led her to a table by the window and they sat looking out.

'It's very busy after the peace of the cemetery,' he said. 'Like somehow coming back to life.'

It seemed a very odd thing to say. Particularly as it wasn't exceptionally busy. But then she thought of some of the curious things she'd said to friends, just to stop them talking about Robert. Telling Gracie that she was thinking of joining the bowls club when she didn't even know whether there was one. She'd seen bowling on TV the day before and it was the first thing that came into her mind. And telling Doreen that she was considering taking up angling.

They chatted about the weather, the traffic and the development of the local supermarket until the tea and cake arrived, was consumed and was long finished. By the time it was time to leave she'd discovered he'd come to England as a boy, and run a small printing firm until he'd retired early to look after his sick wife. He liked opera, how stereotypical she thought, motor cycle racing and collecting model soldiers. He had been born in

9

Milan and his only brother still lived there. He and Sylvia had no children and his birthday was in November. And he'd discovered very little about her.

'Now about the lift,' he said, 'Do you want to take my photo?'

'I hope that's unnecessary.'

'Does that mean you're accepting?'

'Yes, please. Yes, I am. And I'm sorry if I seemed rude earlier.'

'Not at all Mrs Winston.'

'Right, let's be off then.'

They stood. She brushed crumbs from her coat as he paid the bill and they left the tea shop. He led her across the road to where his car was parked. Like Mr Valentino Rossini it was small and tidy. She was slightly disappointed it wasn't a Fiat. It would have been part of the stereotypical Italian.

'Do you want to photograph...?'

'Mr Rossini, my phone doesn't take pictures and like you I have no children.'

'Oh.' He stood silently. 'I'm sorry I didn't mean to intrude.'

'That's alright. I'm sorry I was so abrupt. Shall we get in. And before you suggest the shops or anything, I live at 75 Manchester Street. You may take me home.'

'I might still turn out to be the mad axe man, you know,' he said.

'That's true, Mr Rossini, but then, you see, so might I. We're both taking a chance, aren't we?' He has a nice smile, she thought.

'I don't think your bag is large enough to contain an axe.'

'Not literally,' she said, ' but I could have a....' she was about to say 'dagger' but instead said 'stiletto.'

'Mrs Winston, I am from Milan, not Sicily.'

Apart from giving him directions, the journey was very quiet and uneventful. At length they arrived outside of Mrs Winston's house.

'There you are, safe and sound. Now would you like a lift next Sunday?'

She had had time to think during the short journey. 'Yes please, Mr Rossini. It's a bit cheeky I know but could you possibly collect me from Saint Peter's – say about five past eleven? I'm sorry if that's an inconvenience.'

'No problem. But I have a request?'

Here it comes she thought. So there was an ulterior motive.

'Please stop apologising all the time. It was I who has disrupted your Sunday. I who disturbed you in the cemetery, and I have possibly, after all that, made you late for something this evening. And it is I who have made you nervous.'

'I don't know why you should think..'

'Mrs Winston, you have a habit when you are uncomfortable of stroking your coat.' He imitated her actions.

'Well if that is true,' she was itching to stroke her coat now but resisted, 'I accept your apology. You have been very kind. And I shall look forward to having tea with you next Sunday.' And she realised she meant it.

'My pleasure. Bye bye Mrs Winston.'

'Bye bye, Mr Ross.... Val'

'Thank you Mrs Winston'

'And you may as well know, it's Valerie, although my friends also call me Val.'

They both laughed.

'Bye, bye, Val,' he said.

As he drove off she let herself into the house and put her bags down. Phoenix came to meet her, purring happily at the prospect of food. She realised that because of the disruption to her routine she'd forgotten to put the rubbish from Robert's grave in the bin at the cemetery so she spread it on the kitchen table. There wasn't much, two dog ends for the compost pot, a toffee paper for the recycling pot and a flyer which she smoothed out – September 10th, that was a week on Thursday. It looked bright and cheerful. She wondered how it had got so far from the district where she lived.

Perhaps the organisers were hoping for a big crowd from a wide area. On the back someone had written in Biro what looked like a phone number. She wondered if the phone call had been made before the flyer had been thrown down or dropped. If not, it was too late now. She turned back to the front. She was interested in what it promised. Perhaps now was the time for a change and to start moving on. And it would certainly suit her more than bowling or angling. She smiled at the memory. She clipped the flyer to her fridge with a magnet. She'd nothing else planned for that Thursday. And it did say it was free.

She picked up the empty cat feeding bowl. 'Come on Phoenix, sorry I'm late. Let me feed you and tell you about my day.'

Chapter 2 : Carol's Translation

Carol put down the phone after another rejection. He knew that despite the law he was still being turned down because employers didn't want to employ a foreigner. But dammit, he wasn't a foreigner. He spoke English like a native – better than many, if he was honest. OK, his grandparents had come from Poland as 'displaced persons' after the war and never really learned the language. But he'd been born here. And why, oh why, had his parents given him what turned out to be a girl's name in their adoptive country?

The most recent excuse from an employer was that he was 'over-qualified'. So he couldn't be a stock-controller because he had a degree in IT. Yesterday he'd been turned down as an IT manager because he lacked enough experience. Tomorrow he had an interview in a call centre. He wondered what their excuse would be.

He had been tempted to change his name to Carl. He would have done it years ago but he knew it would have upset his parents and now, even though they were both gone, well now he'd become a bit stubborn.

He looked on the mantel piece for his cigarettes and realised he was down to the last one. Perhaps this was the moment to give up. It would certainly save him a lot of money. And it would be good for his health. On the other hand he had little food in for his evening meal so he had to go out shopping anyway. He might as well pick some up at the same time.

He decided it was still warm enough not to need a coat so left the flat he was living in and set off to walk the couple of blocks to the Brunswick Street shops. Nowicki's, the Polish shop didn't sell tobacco, officially at any rate, so he would buy his groceries from old Mr Nowicki and then nip into the newsagents for his cigarettes.

He liked Mr and Mrs Nowicki. They reminded him of his parents. Neither had fully learned English. Both stressed the importance of their family and religious background. He knew the Nowicki's son was teaching at a university and didn't come home very often and their two daughters were married to 'good catholic husbands.' He vaguely remembered there were some grand children.

As he reached Nowicki's he glanced at the ads in the window. There was the usual cluster advertising rooms, cash in hand jobs and various services by young ladies. It always amused him that if a policeman who spoke Polish ever read them, a number of people, including all the young ladies, would instantly go out of business. And then his eye was caught by an A5 flyer. Apart from its bright colours, it stood out as the only advert in English.

It wasn't for a job, or indeed a young lady, but he thought it might give him a chance to meet local people who might know where there was a job. And after all, he could go for the three weeks free trial it offered and then drop out before paying anything if it didn't suit him.

He went into the shop. Once he'd collected his groceries and was paying Mr Nowicki he casually said, in Polish, 'How does it happen that you have the English poster in the window?'

'Oh,' replied Mr Nowicki,, 'Two very nice young ladies came and asked if they could put it up for two weeks. They looked tired because they had also put some through house doors, so I took pity on them and said 'Yes.' I hope it's not political. I don't wish to be asked questions by the police.'

'Don't you worry, it's not political. Listen and I will tell you the services your ladies are offering.' He then drew Mr Nowicki close to him conspiratorially and whispered in his ear. After a short pause Mr Nowicki who had been prepared to be shocked burst into cheerful laughter. 'You know, young Carol, if you're thinking of going I might even come along myself – but the shop is still open then and I couldn't leave Zofia alone. If you go, you can tell me all about it.'

Carol left the shop and was about to go into the newsagents when he met Mrs Winston coming out. He knew her slightly by sight. She was a school teacher: it had been in all the local press after her husband had been killed in a cycling accident. The lorry driver had been acquitted of dangerous driving and Mrs Winston had been photographed leaving the court in tears. He knew she had not been able to go back to teaching after that and he felt very sorry for her. He didn't think her husband had left her very well off and he didn't know if she got a teacher's pension with giving it up early. But he understood how after it had been in the papers she didn't want to go back. He remembered losing his parents.

'Hello, Mrs Winston'

'Hello – er?'

'Carol – It's a lovely day, isn't it?'

'It is indeed, Carol.' She had no idea who he was. She looked at the t-shirt, jeans and trainers and was again reminded of Robert's views on how a gentleman should dress. But this young gentleman was clean and polite and had a friendly smile. She thought back to her teaching days but couldn't remember a

15

boy called Carol and she was sure she would have done. ' I'm sorry, you'll have to remind me who you are.'

"Oh you don't know me. I just live round here and I often see you about, I have a flat in Jasmine Street and I just wanted to share what a lovely day it was with someone.'

'Well thank you -er- Carol. Oh, of course Carol! After the Pope. You are Polish?'

'Well near enough, My parents were Polish but I am English and I don't think I was named after anyone in particular.'

'I'm sorry, it was rather presumptuous of me.'

'No, not at all,' it was a natural mistake. You are looking different today. Is it a new hairdo?'

'No, don't be silly. I haven't money for such things.'

So Carol's assumption about her financial position was probably right. But he could tell she was pleased by the compliment and he was glad he'd paid it. 'Well something has put a spring in your step. Now you take care. Bye.'

'Bye.' Well! The second unexpected meeting in two days. She smiled. These things usually went in threes. What would tomorrow bring? Or who?

Meanwhile, Carol had reached home and was just putting his key in the lock when he realised that in talking to Mrs Winston he'd forgotten to buy the cigarettes. He let out an expletive that his parents and the Nowickis and probably Mrs Winston, had she spoken Polish, would not have approved of. Well there was one still left in the pack and he couldn't be bothered to go back again.

He went back to his laptop and logged on. He decided to tidy

16

up his website. Web design was not his strength but a university friend had helped him set this up a couple of years ago and he knew how to update it and make changes. But before he did he checked his emails. There were a couple of new ones including a name he didn't recognise.

It was from a Justine Buckley saying she'd seen his website and wondered if he was able to translate Polish things into English. He couldn't see how she could have got that from his website which clearly said he was available to do IT work. He was tempted to write and suggest she use Babelfish but his parents had taught him always to be polite and the lessons held firm. Instead he emailed and said that it wasn't what he was really offering but if there wasn't too much of it he could perhaps undertake it. After a little thought he added that there would be a cost. He sent the email and then settled to revamping his website. Perhaps he really ought to call himself Carl.

Chapter 3: Tamsin's Poster

Tamsin had just finished her drink when Jenny appeared.

'I didn't know what to get you,' she said. She was surprised how ordinary and unglamorous Jenny seemed now she was out of her costume. She guessed, correctly as it turned out, that the other girl was about twenty two. She was not quite as tall as Tamsin with short, pink streaked hair.

It's alright,' replied Jenny, 'I'll order. Same again for you?'

As Tamsin nodded Jenny took a white envelope from her hand bag and slid it across the table, before going to the bar to order the drinks. Tamsin discreetly checked the contents and put it into her own bag. When Jenny returned from the bar Tamsin said, 'Jenny, there's more in the envelope than we agreed.'

'That's because the wedding over-ran. The best man gave me extra for the delay so I split it with you.'

'That's very honest of you.'

'Well I thought you deserved it. I liked your accompaniment, felt it followed the phrasing of my singing.'

'Well you're easy to accompany. And I love your voice.'

'Mm, not everyone thinks I'm easy to accompany. You should have heard – well, never mind. Anyway I've got a couple more weddings coming up next week and the week after. Are you up for them?'

'Love to if I'm available.'

'OK, I'll email you the details. It'll be pretty much the same programme.'

'Are weddings the bulk of your work?'

'No, not at all. I'd starve if that was it. No, I sing at corporate dos – and I have singing pupils and – well bits here and there. And you?'

'Much the same. Monday Tuesday and Wednesday I teach music at Littlestone High and then, like you, it's private pupils and a bit of accompanying. I've been doing it for a couple of years and sometimes wonder whether it's time to move on.'

This seemed to strike a chord with Jenny. 'Move on to what?'

'Oh, I don't know. Perhaps out of music altogether...'

Jenny hesitated for a moment then said, 'I think it would be a great pity if you gave up music. You have a natural talent for accompanying. You know what, I've had half an idea for a year or so and this could be the time. I reckon that with your help we could make it happen.'

'And what's this idea? I'm intrigued.'

'Well, I've lived round here for just over a year and there's quite a strong community feeling but not really any community activities. I thought of starting a community choir.'

'I don't know. How much thought have you given to the detail? Do you think there are enough singers, and how would you pay for rehearsal space and music and stuff.

'I wasn't planning on auditioning or anything like that – just people who fancied having a go at singing.'

'And paying for it?'

'Most people pay for their hobbies. Why not for this. We'd have to do it for free for say the first three weeks to get them in but after that charge – like a sort of evening class. I mean, we'd be up front with people and tell them that it was only the first two or three sessions that were free.'

'And where would this happen?'

'I don't know. Sam, have you got a second?'

The barman came over.

'Sam, do you know anywhere round here where a choir could practice one night a week? Cheap?'

The barman was a young, slightly over-weight, squat man with a cheery face, so useful in a publican. He wrinkled his brow as he thought for a minute, 'How big a choir?'

'No idea,' Jenny smiled. 'Could be as many as thirty'

'Mm,' said Sam, 'Would Thursdays suit you?'

'Yes, I think so..' Jenny saw Tamsin give a quick nod. ' Yes, say eight o'clock to half nine. Why, do you know of somewhere?'

'I'll speak to the boss but I was thinking the room upstairs here. It's not used for very much and is a bit of a wasted space. Want to take a look?'

The Crown had had an interesting history, probably unique among English pubs. It had been built in the early nineteenth century as a Society of Friends meeting house so was basically very simple and unadorned. When the Quaker community had moved out just after the first world war they had sold it to a local food wholesaler. However there were various conditions on the sale, most significant of which was a restriction prohibiting the sale of alcohol. In 1939 the wholesaler moved to bigger premises which had no alcohol restriction. For the next seven years it was used by the army as a depot. The Quaker community were saddened by this and regretted that their predecessors had not legislated against this eventuality as well as the alcohol one. After that it had been used as a temporary school whilst a local one, bombed during World War 2, was rebuilt. Once the children moved back to their rebuilt premises, it was converted to a community centre until the 1980s when the current owner persuaded the local planning officer that the restrictive covenant preventing the sale of alcohol was inconsistent with its primary use as a community centre so when the building was registered at the newly created Land Registry in Leicester there was no mention of it not being allowed to sell alcohol. So it was that Jim Braithwaite bought it and in 1983, on April 21st., Her Majesty The Queen's birthday, it opened its doors and commemorated the date with its name 'The Crown.'

The upstairs room was larger than Jenny had expected, being the whole of the first floor. Her proposed choir would be a bit lost in it. In one corner Sam had stored boxes of crisps and there were a lot of metal stacking chairs along one of the long walls, left over from the days of its use as a community building. Jenny clicked her fingers. The acoustic was OK. Tamsin noted there were a couple of sockets to supply power to her keyboard and although drab, it was well lit and clean.

'And how much would this cost?'

'Well thirty thirsty singers would probably double our takings on a Thursday night so I doubt he'd charge you.'

'Fantastic, can I pop in sometime next week and see what he said?'

'Pop in on Monday lunchtime and you'll be able to talk to him yourself. He comes to check the stock and accounts on a Monday. He's a nice enough bloke. Mr Braithwaite.'

'Cheers, Sam, I owe you one' said Jenny, who was already thinking she could use 'Thirty thirsty singers on a Thursday' as part of her vocal warm up.

The three of them made their way back downstairs. Unlike most pubs, the staircase was quite wide, a testament to the foresight of the original builders.

'And now Tamsin – questions?'

'Well where exactly do I fit in?'

'Ah, your mission, should you choose to accept it, is to bring your keyboard and accompany for me. And you can help with publicity and admin and all of that. And we'd split the money if it got going'

'And how will you get people involved?'

'If you build it, they will come.' Jenny smiled. ' But more practically we need to design a flyer and post it in as many shops and libraries and places and push it through doors and...'

'Hang on, who's going to do all this?'

'Well I think that's down to you and me.'

'And when do you want this choir to actually start?'

'I was thinking two weeks on Thursday.'

'I see,' said Tamsin. She sipped her drink thoughtfully.

Jenny sensed a lack of enthusiasm in her colleague. 'We could make it happen you know.'

'Not by two weeks on Thursday we couldn't. Not if we spend the rest of tonight sitting in this pub drinking. We need to get back to my place and start designing these flyers. And soon.'

'Does that mean you're up for it?'

'Finish your drink and let's get going.'

Jenny had only met Tamsin that afternoon. Her regular pianist had inconsiderately gone on holiday for a month and that left her with no-one to play for three weddings. Luckily, a friend of a friend of a friend had given her Tamsin's contact details and Tamsin had been more than adequate. In fact, they'd struck up an immediate musical rapport. With only half an hour's prep before the gig, Jenny knew she had found an accompanist who suited her style. Now it seemed she'd been able to share her vision for a community choir. She thought Tamsin was 25, which made her three years older than she was; old enough to have a little experience but young enough still to have the energy and enthusiasm.

Once they reached Tamsin's flat Jenny realised she'd met her soul-mate. They obviously shared the same tastes in furniture and décor. Tamsin offered her tea, not the thick brown stuff with milk and sugar her parents had brought her up on in her native Yorkshire but subtle Thai herbal tea. And a glance round the kitchen indicated a fellow vegetarian.

As soon as they started work on the poster, Jenny realised she'd also found someone with a natural talent for publicity. The first word Tamsin wanted on the poster was not choir, or music but FREE. Free loan of music. Free opportunity to sing. Free chance to make new friends.

'If we are doing three weeks for free, let's tell 'em it's free,' Tamsin argued. By eleven that night it was done. Tamsin had a copy of the poster on her computer and had emailed a copy to Jenny's.

'What now?' she said.

'I've got a couple of dozen arrangements of different Christmassy stuff. I'll get it photocopied up. And I'll prepare practice files.'

'I meant what about the posters. Are we going to run off 50 each?'

'No, I don't think so, Tam. If the pub's OK with us practising there I'll get a thousand printed. Let's start as we mean to go on, with professional standards. If we can get thirty singers, I reckon we can break even by Christmas. I'll cover the costs until then.'

Jenny left Tamsin's flat with a song in her heart. At long last she had started the ball rolling on her idea.

Tamsin prepared for bed little knowing what she had helped to start but inspired by the enthusiasm of her new found friend.

Chapter 4: Richard's Notes

Richard hated Thursdays. He disliked Mondays, Tuesdays, Wednesdays and Fridays, but he hated Thursdays with a passion normally reserved for serial murderers, child molesters and white van drivers who didn't see motorcyclists because they were on their mobile phones. He hadn't always hated Thursdays. He could remember a time before his accident, before he became a teacher when he quite liked them. Fridays Saturdays and Sundays were usually good for live gigs and mid-week was when he recorded. But then he'd had the accident and even though he was now allegedly 'back to normal' he knew he had lost that edge that had brought him the work playing bass for decent bands.

So he stopped being one of 'Toxic Wasters' and became Mr Carlston who taught music. Only he didn't. Well not very much. In the three years he'd been at Brunswick High the results had gone down. The novelty of having an ex-pop star on the staff had worn off fairly quickly. Music theory bored him. The kids all wanted to be pop stars but weren't prepared to put in the sheer hard graft of learning their instrument, not just to being good enough but to the level of being better than every other wannabe. And there was yet another Ofsted inspection looming in the near future.

He turned over in bed.

Mr Thomas, the head had suggested he start a choir. He knew why. Choirs were cheap. You didn't need expensive instruments. You certainly didn't need amplifiers. And they had choirs in Wales. And if St David ever gave up the job, Mr Thomas was odds on favourite to become the next patron saint of Wales.

But it wasn't just the music. He now had 3 periods of English to teach a week as well. Ever since Mrs Winston left because she couldn't face the staff or the kids after her husband got killed. Well he couldn't face the staff or kids either. He'd phone in sick. He wondered how long he could get away with that. Probably not very long. Actually, probably not at all. Apart from being Welsh Mr Thomas was also quite shrewd. That's probably why he'd become a head.

Should he get up and shave. He'd given up his beard when he'd started teaching but perhaps a change would help him kick-start his life. Not that he'd kick started any thing since the accident.

He swung himself out of bed. If only it had been any other day but Thursday. Actually there was something significant about Thursday, if he could remember. He was in the shower before it came to him. Next week was the night those young women were starting their community choir down the pub. He was tempted to go. Show them how a professional musician worked. Though there wouldn't be much call for a bass guitarist even if he had appeared on TV a number of times. And when people pressed him about exactly how many times he'd been on TV he always told them that three was a number.

But they were good looking women. Fit. He missed the fans from the old days. He always had a number of attractive women to pick from; and yes, OK, three was still a number. He was aware that a couple of the older girls at Brunswick High had crushes on him, but that was asking for trouble. But those two intense young women with their missionary zeal for their choir – they were something else. Unless they turned out to be dykes, of course. You never could tell.

He felt the stubble on his chin. Yes, time to grow the beard again. He made his first coffee of the day. He looked at the tweed sports jacket he normally wore to work and thought, 'No. Not today. Today would be denim jeans and a leather jacket. Mr Thomas would hate it.' He thought about Kes, the set work he had to teach after dinner. He'd never actually read it, but he'd seen the film years ago. That probably meant he knew more about it than 4b. He wished he could remember those choir girls' names. He thought one was a Jenny. That was the younger one. He thought he'd recognised the older one but he couldn't place her. Oh well, that was recreational chemicals for you. Old habits die hard.

Chapter 5: Colin's Gospel

Sam took a last look round the bar. Nobody was waiting to be served. It was the usual slack Tuesday lunchtime. If things didn't improve soon he reckoned he'd be looking for another job. Pubs were closing left, right and centre and there was no reason to think The Crown would not soon follow them into oblivion. He slipped into the back room where Mr Braithwaite was waiting.

'OK, Sam, what's this idea?'

'Well there's these two women want to set up a choir on Thursday evenings and I thought if we gave them the upstairs room they would bring thirty thirsty...'

'Gave?' Mr Braithwaite looked troubled. 'Gave?'

'I don't think they'd be able to afford it if we tried to charge.'

'Two women, you said? Young? Pretty?'

'What's that got to do with anything?'

'Come on, Sam, I know you.'

'Well, yes.'

'Thought so!'

'No, listen Mr Braithwaite, one of them's coming in in a minute – she's hoping to see you. At least let her pitch her idea.'

'Well you're right the Crown does need a shot in the arm but it'll take more than thirty warblers on a Thursday evening.'

They were interrupted by a ping from the bar.

'That'll be her,' said Sam.

But it wasn't. A tall, thin, darkly dressed, miserable looking man stood at the bar.

'Ah there you are, Sam,' came a deep, sepulchral voice.

'Hello Colin, what can I do for you?'

'It's that time of the year again. Could you put this up for me.' He handed over a poster.

'That'll be OK, Colin, now what can I get you?'

'Well I wasn't going to...'

'The boss is in the back,' said Sam significantly.

'In that case, half a pint of your best bitter, please,' said Colin, taking the hint.

'Sorry, am I late?' Jenny burst into the bar.

'No, Mr Braithwaite's still here.' Sam called, 'Mr Braithwaite, your visitor is here.' He turned back and gave Jenny the thumbs down sign before handing Colin his drink. Colin settled himself on the bar stool.

'Hello,' said Mr Braithwaite, 'I'm Jim Braithwaite and you are?'

'Jenny Lint, and it's very good of you to see me Mr Braithwaite.' She saw a stocky, no nonsense business man in a navy suit. He saw a small, sparky young woman. No wonder Sam had given her the time of day.

'Sam says you want to start a choir?'

'Yes.'

'Here?'

'Yes'

'Why?'

'Because this area needs a community group to pull it all together and because being in a choir is something anyone can do – and singing is something I'm passionate about. And we're just going to try it for free for three weeks to see if it works.' She knew she was beginning to gabble.

'Mm. And what's in it for The Crown?'

'Well, without being rude, look around.'

The tall man with the half pint glass shuffled uncomfortably as their eyes examined the almost empty bar. 'Wouldn't thirty people be better than this.'

'This is Tuesday lunchtime.'

'True, But Thursday evenings are even quieter.' Jenny realised she may have gone too far.

'You're a bit blunt.,

'Sorry.'

'No. don't apologise. Where I come from, Barnsley, we like blunt. I don't suppose you've ever even heard of Barnsley?'

'Mr Braithwaite, I was born and raised in Wakefield and one of my first gigs was singing in 'Annie' in the Lamproom at Barnsley.'

'Annie, is that the one about the ginger lass in the orphanage?'

'That's the one.'

'About thirteen years ago?'

'About that.'

'Blimey. My wife took me to see that. Her friend, Mrs Kay or something, was the woman who ran the orphanage.'

'Irene Cadeby?'

'Aye, that'd be her. And you were the little ginger lass?' He looked pointedly at her pink streaked hair.

'It was a wig, Mr Braithwaite.'

'Well, who would have believed it? What a small world. Well, Miss – Ms -Lund – if you're just talking three weeks I suppose I could give it a go. After all, we might none of us be here after that. OK, you can use the upstairs room for the first three weeks of your warblers. Then, if there's anything to talk about we'll talk again. But I'd lay odds you won't get thirty – or even twenty. I know this neighbourhood. If they won't come in here to drink, they certainly won't come in to sing. Still, I wish you luck anyway. It's been interesting meeting you.'

He offered his hand which she shook. 'Good-bye and good luck.'

And before she had time to answer he was gone, shouting, 'Bye Sam' as the door swung to behind him.

Sam came through from the back. ' Well you've certainly got the gift of the gab. I would have put money on him turning you down.'

The tall man had finished his drink and stood up. 'Excuse me,' he intoned,' I couldn't help overhearing your conversation.'

Jenny beamed, 'And you are a tenor looking for a choir to join?'

'Regretfully no, but I may be able to help in another way.'

Jenny waited.

'If you get your choir – and unlike Mr Braithwaite, I have faith in this community and think you might, have you thought where they will eventually perform?'

'You're not going to tell me you're a TV producer?'

'I'm not. Come with me.'

'Where?'

'Please come with me – we'll be back in ten minutes, Sam, and Ms Lunt will buy me another half'

'Hang on,' started Jenny.

'Just humour him,' said Sam,' you'll be OK.'

By now Colin was by the door waiting for her so Jenny followed him out. She cast a despairing glance back at Sam, just in time to see him smirk. What was going on?

Colin strode purposefully across the road and up to the entrance of the church which stood looking forlornly down on the street and proclaiming itself to be 'The Parish Church of St Peter.'

'Why are we coming to the church? It's not Sunday, it will be shut.'

'Sadly that is true,' said Colin, 'but I have the keys of St Peter's.' The joke was wasted, as he had known it would be.

He removed from his pocket a huge key which he used to unlock the massive door. She imagined him as a medieval monk opening up this holy place for her and other pilgrims, an illusion immediately shattered when he said, 'Just wait there a moment while I switch the alarm off.'

She heard the tell tale bleeps as he disarmed an alarm system, then he beckoned her in.

'Are you the..' she wasn't sure if the correct word was vicar.

'I am the Priest in Charge here, but people call me Colin. It is my Christian name.'

'You're not wearing a …,' she gestured around her throat.

'A dog-collar? No, I don't usually. It sometimes puts people off.'

'Why have you brought me here?'

'I asked where your choir would perform. Now for thirty, perhaps twenty, this is too large, but come, let me show you the Lady Chapel.'

The church was immense and, even at lunchtime, gloomy. She clicked her fingers and heard the sound rebound around the walls. At least it wouldn't be difficult to sing in but it smelled dusty and unused. She followed him along the main church and through an arch.

The transformation was magical. Whilst the rest of the church was imposing in a dark, gothic sort of way, the Chapel was sun-lit, intimate and welcoming.

'This is beautiful,' Jenny whispered.

'It is. And I would have offered it to you for rehearsals but it is too cold once the autumn arrives. We can barely afford to warm it for our own worship I'm afraid. But for a single concert we could perhaps come to some arrangement.'

'I'm sorry Colin, but I'd better explain. I'm not a Christian.'

'I'd guessed that,' he replied. 'You're obviously unfamiliar with our terminology. But don't worry. Jesus' own disciples were not Christians when they first came to know him.'

'Yes, but many of the people from this neighbourhood who may join the choir could be from other religions.'

'But they are neighbours. And when Jesus was asked, who is my neighbour he told them a story.'

'OK, but we won't be singing hymns – well perhaps the odd gospel – or perhaps a carol.'

'That is your choice. And probably a very good one. If you sang only hymns I think your choir would end up like ours. Gone.'

'Well, Colin, it's a lovely offer and if we ever do get a choir and reach a stage when we are ready to give a concert I will speak to you again if I may.'

'Of course.'

'How do I get in touch with you?'

'On the board outside it gives my phone and times of the services.'

'Sorry, I didn't notice.'

'Few do.'

Jenny realised she was beginning to feel sorry for this gaunt man in his gaunt church.

'Well let's hope they read my flyer. When they're printed may I put one on your notice-board?'

'Of course – please don't cover up my details or the times of services. Or the poster advertising our Harvest Festival which, by the way, was why I was in the pub at lunchtime. It's a week on Sunday. I don't suppose I can interest you..?'

'Thank you, you've been very kind. I'm afraid I can't do Sunday but perhaps one day I can do something for you.'

'There is one thing you can do for me today. When you get home, go on to the internet and read the story in St Luke's gospel chapter ten verse twenty-nine. And may the Lord help with your recruiting.'

'Thank you. Thirty would be good but twenty would be enough, fifteen at a pinch.'

'Build it and they will come.' He smiled, 'and that's not from the Bible.'

Chapter 6 : Barbara's Menus

Barbara thrived on routine.

7.30 Rise and shine. Or at least rise.

8:30 Get the kids off to school and the washing and cleaning done. Ironing used to be included but she'd realised that nobody really cared if stuff got pressed.

11.35 Catch the 42A bus to the cafe where she worked.

12:00 Work at the Cafe.

2.30 Lunch break. Shop for groceries and clothes, pay bills etc.

3.15 Back at the cafe

6.30 Leave work to catch the 6.35 42A home.

7.00 Home and prepare dinner while the kids, Howie and Debbie, did homework or played computer games.

9.30 Kids in bed and washing up done

10.00 Bed

Once every three weeks the kids went to their dad's so she could do a Saturday and Sunday shift at the cafe.

This Monday was just as usual. The cafe wasn't busy and Tina, the other assistant was rearranging the biscuit shelf when she arrived.

'Hiya, Barbara,' she said, 'not much doing today.'

'Any of the regulars been in yet?'

'Mm,' said Tina. ' The three girls from the supermarket came over for a coffee. We might be losing them though 'cos the supermarket's installing a kitchen where they can make their own. And that funny bald-headed bloke with the bike was in. Oh and Prince Charles.'

Prince Charles was in reality a middle-aged man with prominent ears and a fairly posh voice. Barbara and Tina didn't know his real name but he regularly called in for tea and biscuits.

'So what did you get up to at the weekend, then?' Tina knew that Barbara's weekends were, if anything, less exciting than her own.

'Oh, the usual. On Friday I went to the opera, then on Saturday I went hang-gliding. On Sunday we played polo at Windsor. What about you?'

'Oh, well it was my weekend here. The Duchess of Cambridge popped in on Saturday and Johnny Depp on Sunday. He wants to shoot some of the scenes for his new movie in a typical English Cafe and he thought we'd do.'

Barbara's eyebrows went up. ' You are still kidding, aren't you?'

'Course I am. It was just the usual weekend mixture.' Mrs Greencote won't be in for a couple of weeks. She's going to be in hospital, something to do with her legs. And Mr Pinley, you know, him that walks with a stick and always wears a flat cap. His daughter's expecting again. Oh and big news, that nice Italian gentleman, Mr Rossini, came in and he has a lady friend.'

'I thought he was married.'

'No, his wife died a couple of years ago. That's why he comes here on a Sunday. To visit her grave next door. Anyway, back to work.'

The door had opened and a group of customers came in.

 For the next hour they were busy. It was obvious from the snippets they overheard that there had just been a funeral in the cemetery next door. This was a splinter group who were not going to the reception at the Sultan of Egypt but just wanted a cup of tea before dashing off back to their various homes or work places. Eventually, bit by bit the cafe emptied.

Eventually a tall dark man came. He came to the counter and ordered a cup of tea and a chicken sandwich. He went and sat at the corner table and produced a small black book. He found a bookmarked page and started to read.

Tina made the tea while Barbara produced the sandwich. When they took him his order he thanked them and returned to his reading..

'Shall I do us both a cuppa,' Tina asked.

'Yes, go on then.'

'You know it's my Gary's birthday next week?'

'Is it? How old is he now?'

'He'll be ten.'

'Are you doing anything special?'

'He wants a sleepover. Would your two like to come?'

'I don't know. I can ask them. Which day is it?'

'Thursday. A week on Thursday. Joe'll pick 'em up and you can have an evening off.'

'That would be lovely, I'll see if they want to come.'

'You know, you need a regular time for yourself.'

'With two kids? You must be joking.'

'Well get their dad to help out more.'

'You don't know Ken. It's bad enough sorting out his weekends. He can never remember which one I'm working.'

'But if it was, say, every Thursday it would be easy.'

'Like I say, you don't know Ken. Anyway, back to work.' A mother with two children was struggling in with a push chair. I know the feeling, thought Barbara. The tall guy had stood up and held the door for the woman before leaving.

 By half past six when she and Tina were locking up, Barbara had agreed to phone Ken and see if they could arrange something. She'd also agreed that any free time she got as a result was too valuable to waste on catching up with

38

housework.

The bus was crowded and she realised she hadn't planned the evening meal. Well it would have to be fish fingers and chips again. At least she had some fresh vegetables.

She thought back to her wedding reception. Tony, Ken's best man, had told the joke about buying a Divorcee Barbie Doll which was expensive because it came with Ken's car, Ken's house and so on. Well she'd news for Tony. The house was rented, the car non-existent. All this divorcee Barbie came with was Ken's Kids.

As she walked from the bus stop she thought that despite all the worry they brought her, she couldn't imagine life without them. They went to an after school club and usually got home about the same time as she did. She'd never wanted them to be latch-key children but you didn't always get what you wanted in this life.

Having Thursday nights off seemed very attractive. Whatever she planned to do with it. She rather fancied taking up an art class. That way she'd meet up with other adults. And painting looked very relaxing. She opened the front door and yelled, 'Hello kids, I'm home.' Two heads looked over the banister as she picked up the post and leaflets from the mat. She wondered how the kids managed to step over the post without noticing it.

'Hiya, mum, what's for tea?'

'Oh let me get my coat off. Then it'll be fish-fingers and chips.' The heads disappeared.

She looked at the post. Gas bill. Letter from her brother in New Zealand. Council Tax Bill. Leaflet advertising Broadband and another advertising a new choir. Note from the council saying the bin collections were changing days. She looked again at the choir leaflet. It was upstairs at the local pub so it was easy to get to but more importantly it was free. Art class wouldn't be. And it was on a Thursday. Sometimes things were just fate. She turned the grill on and got the chips and fish fingers from the freezer. She shouted up the stairs, 'Howie, Debbie do you want to go to a sleepover at Tina's? It's Gary's birthday.' She counted the delighted squeals from upstairs as a 'yes.' She'd have to sort out a card and a present.

As she prepared carrots and runner beans she wondered how Ken would react to her request for him to baby-sit, because she knew that was what it really was. And more to the point, how would Emma, Ken's latest, take it? Well there was only one way to find out. After tea she dialled his number.

Chapter 7 Colette's Diary

Septrmber 3rd

Mr Carlston took us for English this afternoon. He was telling us about this book. 'Kes.'

I think he might be going to grow a beard. He'll look fantastic with a goatee. He looks fantastic already. Today he was wearing a black leather jacket and denim jeans. Like he used to wear when he was with his band, Actually, he was also wearing odd socks. When my dad does that, my mother makes him go and change them. She says it reflects badly on her as his wife. Mr Carston obviously doesn't have a wife. He needs one. He's only about 7 years older than me, I think. When we asked how old he was last year, he told us he was only 21 but teaching us had aged him.

When I told him I couldn't find the page he came and leaned over me. I could feel his warm breath on my neck. And when Hermione Smyth told him she couldn't find her page either he just asked Tom Clancy to find it for her. Ha. She hates Tom Clancy. We all do.

He asked us about the title character and when I said 'It's a bird, sir,' I got one of his special smiles and he said, 'Well done, Colette' in that sexy voice he sometimes uses. And I only guessed the answer because there was a picture of a bird on the cover.

Mr Thomas says that Mr Carlston is going to start a choir. At least I think Mr Thomas was suggesting that Mr Carlston should. If he does I'll join it. Singing's a bit of a laugh. And Hermione Smyth sounds like a tortoise when she sings.

When Mr Carlston was in a band he was called Shaggzz. I wonder why? My mum said she thought he did drugs, but that's not true or they wouldn't have let him be a teacher. And anyway, that's not so bad. My mum does cider. And fags. She stinks of fags. Hermione Smyth does fags as well. She reckons it makes her look cool. You could cover her in ice and she still wouldn't look cool. Serves her right if she ends up with cancer.

Sometimes Mr Carlston sings in class but it's not as good as when you hear his CDs or see him on Youtube. He only sings in class when we're doing music. Not when we're doing English.

When he did English with us today he forget to set us any homework. I went to the staff room after school to remind him but Miss Kendrick said he'd already gone. I don't think that it was true because I think Miss Kendrick fancies him herself and doesn't want competition. But she's well old. Megan Law says she goes to her mum's salon to have her hair done and she told her mum she's nearly thirty.

I told mum they might be starting a choir at school and if they did I might join it. She said that they're starting one at the pub. There was a leaflet through the door. She gave it me. I didn't tell her that it weren't the singing that attracted me.

I found Shaggzz's facebook page and messaged him that I wanted to be a friend. He hasn't answered yet.

There's some dead good pictures of him when he was in his band and lots about how to get his CDs and stuff. I've already got a poster up in my bedroom. There's nothing about how he's turned into Mr Carlston but I googled him and found out how he'd been on his motorbike and this van driver drove in front of him and both his arms were damaged and he has never played again. And it's dead romantic.

But it's not true because he often plays his guitar in our music lessons. He reckons he's no longer good enough to play professionally but I don't think that's true. Perhaps it's to do with insurance or something. Perhaps he just needs the right person to give him his confidence back.

I've put some nice photos of me on holiday in Brighton on my Facebook page. If he becomes my friend he'll see them. I've got the yellow and blue bikini on. I got a lad on the beach to take the pictures. He wanted me to take my top off but I'm not stupid. He gave me his phone number but I'll not use it. I gave him mine, only it wasn't, it was Hermione Smyth's. It's a pity I don't know Miss Kendrick's. I could have given him hers.

Mr Carlston has letters after his name. They are BA. I googled it. It means Bachelor of Arts. The arts bit probably means he does paintings like Mr Thicket. And the Bachelor bit means he's not married so that's OK.

If he's an artist perhaps I could be his model. If he accepts my friend request and sees my picture perhaps he'll suggest it. I'd take my top off for him. I've even got that Kes book for him from the library to read although if you ask me it's dead boring.

Chapter 8 : Kim's Assessment

Kim got into her car and tossed her back pack on the passenger seat beside her.

The classes had gone well tonight. The tiny tots had remembered all their steps from the previous week, the intermediates were beginning to look like dancers and the seniors were ready to perform. The problem was their regular booking had been cancelled.

Normally this was the season when Kim was beginning to think about choreographing the local pantomime but this year Cinderella was not going to the ball. Or more accurately the local council had stopped the ball. Apparently they'd doubled the rent of the Civic Centre and the Brunswick Players could no longer afford it.

She had considered promoting her own show but didn't think she could afford to. Booking a reasonable small theatre was very expensive.

As usual, the vicar of St Peter's had offered his huge barn of a church but it was cold and cheerless and the cost of temporary lighting was prohibitive. Kim was already forced to supplement her income with two days a week at the new supermarket working on the check out but it wasn't ideal, particularly when her dance pupils came in. And the manager was pushing her to do a Saturday shift which was when most of her pupils could come for lessons.

She'd been teaching dance for nearly four years now and hoped to be more successful than she was. Before moving to the city, she had done a couple of stints on cruise ships but she found that restrictive and exhausting without giving her a lot of satisfaction. All her students did well in exams and the annual pantomime had not only been a useful extra income but also allowed her to showcase her talents as both a teacher and a choreographer.

And it wasn't just the dancing that depressed her. Her social life wasn't up to much. It was a couple of years since she'd been in a serious relationship. She had little in common with he work colleagues at the supermarket and she couldn't really afford to go out socialising.

She'd picked up a flyer about a new choir starting and thought she might give it a go. It could be an opportunity to network with some other creatives. And the leaflet said it was free for the first three weeks so she had nothing to lose. She'd seen the two girls who'd delivered it and they looked about her age so it wasn't going to be a lot of OAPs singing Mozart. And they met in a pub!

She put on her belt, started the engine and pulled out into the traffic. Usually she liked the impersonality of the big city but tonight she missed her childhood home. Once she got in she'd phone her mum. She was now her best friend, despite the arguments they'd had as she grew up in Rugby. If only teenagers could see ten years into the future. But then when she'd been a teenager she thought she actually could so presumably all teenagers felt like that. A couple of her older dancers obviously had difficult relationships with their parents. Still, she was a dance teacher not a social worker or psychiatrist.

As she crawled along in the traffic, she reflected that the rent was due again and repairing a dent in her car had left a more noticeable dent in her credit card. A couple of her friends had paid their student fees working at a lap dancing club across town but she couldn't see herself going down that route. She felt the approach of one or two passengers on the last cruise ship had been pretty degrading so what it would be like...No, better not think of that.

The slow moving traffic had now ground to a halt. She could see temporary traffic lights a few cars ahead.

The trouble was that apart from dancing she had no marketable skills. OK she could work the tills at the supermarket. Big deal. She could drive. In fact she had tried using her driving skills to work for a small parcels delivery firm but the pay was pretty awful and that's how the car had got its dent – even though it had been properly parked while she was delivering a package.

An irritating horn sounded behind her urging her to close the ten metre gap that had opened between her and the small van in front of her.

She had jealously guarded her contact with the pantomime organisers to prevent other dance groups stealing her pitch so she wasn't surprised not to be able to break into other shows. Other dance teachers were just as protective.

She was on the move again and through the roadworks.

She had suggested running after-school classes at a couple of local schools, but they could only offer her a room to rent at a far more expensive rate than the hall she currently hired at the baptist church. She wondered about entering something for one of the TV talent shows but realised she would be one of thousands of dance teachers with the same idea. What she needed was a big concept with high impact value – something like Riverdance. But, lovely as they were, she couldn't see Kimz Kidz in that league. Although, without the pantomime, it

46

would give them something to focus on. Perhaps a Christmas based dance drama.

Or perhaps moving back to Rugby might be a plan. She knew her mum would be delighted to have her back and she could live rent free. But the thought of giving up on all the work she had put into building up Kimz Kidz didn't appeal. And if she moved back to Rugby, then what. Full time in a supermarket. At least she wouldn't spend all this time stuck in traffic.

Being realistic she decided to give it till Christmas. By then she might be bankrupt and have no other choice.

Chapter 9 : Sara's photos

Sara poured herself another cup of coffee. Mark was gone. After nearly a year. She looked round the flat. He'd taken his books. All of them. And his CDs but that wasn't too bad. She had the ones she wanted on her lap-top. He'd taken his pans. That was more of a problem. She would have to learn to cook again. And he'd taken the picture of Aegina. She wasn't sure about that. That's where they'd met. Was that to remember her by? Or was it to stop her thinking about him. Or was he thinking of going back there. She tasted the coffee, remembering the beach, the sand, the warmth and the first moment she'd seen him.

He'd been sitting on a wall reading. He looked as though he spent more time surfing or playing sport but there he was with a book. She walked past him. Twice. He didn't look up or notice her. She went and sat on the wall and took out her phone. She took several pictures of the empty beach. She took more of the empty sea. Eventually she spoke. 'Would you mind if I took a picture of you?'

'I'm sorry?' He looked up for the first time.

'I didn't mean to disturb you. May I take a picture of you?'

'If you want. Why?'

'Well there's nothing else, much, is there? Apart from sand and sea. And sky.'

'That depends'. He shut his book. 'Just come over here.' He led her to the edge of the water. Now, what can you see?'

'Water? Oh, just a minute', something like a shadow was moving near the edge, 'Is that a jelly fish?'

'It is. Quite a small one.'

'Looks big enough to me'.

For the next five minutes he spoke knowledgeably and entertainingly about jelly-fish. Sara learnt that some were edible, some as big as she was, that jelly-fish were around before dinosaurs, that they have no brain, and a group of jellyfish is called a smack. She was warned against the group called medusae, which sting. He was just embarking on an explanation of the life cycle of the jelly-fish when he stopped and pointed to an object further up the beach.

'There, look, a sea-turtle', and he set off along the beach. Sara was rather hoping that she would not get another natural history lesson but this time he explained how one of the earliest mints in the world had been on Aegina and the earliest coins had depicted turtles.

While she was still digesting this nugget he took her hand and drew her to the top of the beach behind where she had found him. 'Now what can you see?'

Apart from a few small buildings she could see no wild-life.

'Nothing, I don't think,' she said.

'Ah, well I can see a bar. Would you like a drink.?'

As they walked he asked how she came to be on her own. She explained she was with three friends who had gone for a walk across the island but she had a hangover from last night. He asked if one of them was a tall, noisy auburn haired one and she asked how he knew and he said all four of them ought to have hangovers. Most of the residents had heard them coming back from the local bar in the early hours of the morning.

He told her he was doing marine biology at Imperial so this was a sort of working holiday. She explained she worked in a shoe shop. She didn't mention that she occasionally played guitar and sang at folk clubs.

After the drink she thought it was time to go back to the hotel for her friends and he said, 'See you.'

It was only when she met up with Celine, Kate and Samira and was sharing the story of the meeting that she realised they'd not told each other their names.

The four girls had booked a boat trip for the following day and the day after that they were due to leave. Sara half hoped to see the young man either on the boat back to the mainland or on the flight from Athens but it didn't turn out like that.

About a fortnight after settling back into the shop routine she was phoned by her older sister Helen who wondered if Auntie

Sara would like to take her 5 year old nephew out for the day whilst Helen went into the city shopping. After some discussion it was agreed that they would meet in town, Helen would go and do her shopping while Sara would take Harry to the aquarium. When they arrived at the aquarium they signed up for the 'Kiddy Tour' with Davy Jones.

And who should turn out to be Davy Jones but the young man from Aegina, resplendent in tricorn hat, eye-patch and full pirate costume. She took great pains to introduce herself as Sara and her nephew, slight emphasis on the word 'nephew', Harry.

Davy was just as enthralling teaching 5 year olds about the various sea creatures as he had been teaching her about jelly fish. At the end of the tour there was a little competition which all the children won, and each received a sea-horse shaped lollipop.

Then there was a question for the adults. 'What is the collective name for a group of jelly-fish?'. She was certain he hadn't mentioned it in the tour but she remembered. 'Smack', she blurted out.

'Well done,' said Davy. 'If you hang on I have a small prize for you. The rest of you, thank you for being such wonderful visitors to our aquarium. Please come again. And tell your friends.'

'And now, Sara, your prize.' He reached behind the counter and produced a small box of chocolate liqueurs. Before she had time to wonder why he kept a box of chocolates in reception he said, 'My real name is Mark, by the way.'

'Not Davy Jones?'.

'No, Mark Stephenson. Davy Jones is whoever is wearing the costume. It helps pay the bills. Now I've finished for the morning I'm gasping for a cup of coffee. Would you and Harry like to join me?'

'Shall we go to the cafe here?' she asked.

'Not on what they pay me. I know a nice place round the corner.'

'Well if you've time.' By now Mark had removed the hat and put it on Harry who wasn't impressed, opened a locker and put the coat, eye-patch and hat into it and had put his own jacket on.

'Did you enjoy the rest of your holiday?' she asked.

'Yes I did. Look what are your plans for Friday?'

'I finish work at 4.30. Then I'm free. Why?'

'In that case would you like to come to the cinema with me?'

'That depends. If it's Jaws, or 20,000 leagues under the sea…' She smiled.

'Actually it's Finding Nemo. No I'm joking. You can pick.'

By now they had reached the cafe and the next twenty-five minutes were spent on sorting Harry and themselves food and drink. As they were about to leave Mark produced a leaflet from The Aquarium and a pen.

'Mark, can I be really honest, I'm not that into fish.'

Mark laughed and wrote on the back of the leaflet. 'We have to leave our phones in the security box at work. I was so keen to get you a coffee I forgot to pick it up. Here's my phone number. Ring me on Thursday and tell me where we're going.

51

Must go now. Duty calls. Argh argh me Hearties'.

'I liked him', said Harry as Mark disappeared back to the aquarium.

'Me too,' said Sara.

She had another sip of her wine. Almost a year ago. She remembered the panic when she'd got home and couldn't find the phone number and having to phone him at the aquarium. And things had gone well at the cinema, and after. And bit by bit Mark moved into her life and then into her flat.

She remembered their first quarrel. Mark had lost some university papers and she got the blame for the state the flat was in and she told him that he could always help by tidying and cleaning as he was virtually living there anyway. They'd made up after that but there were other arguments. It turned out he didn't like folk music and wouldn't be seen dead in a folk club.

And then he'd graduated.

She realised they had never discussed what would happen when he stopped being a student. She didn't imagine marine biologists were in great demand. But a letter had come. Did he want a two year contract in Iceland. And he'd said he was going. She was welcome to go with him. And the argument had started. She didn't like the cold, she didn't want to give up her career, and she really didn't like bloody fish.

So now, here she was on her own again. And the coffee was finished. She decided that as the Sunday morning weather was nice she would go for a walk. She had a regular route up the main road, past the cafe, through the cemetery and, if necessary, into the supermarket. She put some bird seed into a bag and put it in a pocket. Sometimes she would stop briefly in the cemetery and feed the birds and the squirrels.

She set her house alarm and as she closed the front door she noticed a leaflet sticking out of it. She pulled it out and glanced at it. It was for some free choir. She stuffed it in her pocket so that she could recycle it when she got home.

Chapter 10 : Pauline's Prescription

The day ward record said that Nurse Phillips had collapsed at 19:47 yesterday. Pauline wasn't surprised. As things were she thought it wouldn't be long before others started dropping. She knew which one Nurse Phillips was: the white girl who regularly worked the men's day ward. She'd been heavily pregnant last time she'd seen her. Well she wouldn't be working men's day ward for a while. Pauline checked the list for today. There were two overnighters who would be coming back shortly, then 10 on the morning list and another 10 for the afternoon.

At 20 to 8 the first of the overnighters was brought in. Although he was in a wheelchair she thought he'd be discharged and out well before lunchtime.

'Good Morning, Mr..' she checked her notes, ' Prentice. And how are you today?'

'I'm fine, thank you, nurse. Doctor said that once I could pee OK I could go home. And I can.'

'Good, well we'll just let the Doctor check you and then sort out discharging you.' After six months on geriatrics this emergency shift to cover mens' day ward was already looking good.

'Missed all the excitement yesterday, didn't you?' Mr Prentice was obviously dying to fill her in on the events of the night before.

'Now Mr Prentice, we don't gossip about you patients so I'll thank you not to start gossiping about the nurses.' She was saved from further discussion by the arrival of Mr Cornish. He didn't look so good. For a start he was on a trolley.

'Not as bad as he looks.' It was Mr Prentice again. 'He was last one in last night – for his op I mean, and Nurse Phillips said he'd not reacted well to the anaesthetic. That was before she keeled over of course. I didn't know what to do so I pressed an alarm and doctors and people came and took her away. The Doctor fellow said it was worse than A&E in here. I don't reckon she should have been working in her condition. She was very pregnant. And she was already on duty here when I got here at half past eight in the morning.'

'Would you like a cup of tea?' Pauline asked, hoping to stem the flow of conversation.

'Well, only if you've got time. We don't want another of you keeling over. Hello Mr Cornish, are you feeling a bit better today? It's funny, nurse, isn't it: him being called Cornish when he comes from Somerset.'

By now Pauline and the porter who had brought him had

managed to transfer Mr Cornish from the trolley to a bed. Mr Cornish had helped quite a bit. He was far more conscious than she had first thought.

'Morning, Mick'. This time Mr Prentice was addressing the ward auxiliary who had just arrived in blue coveralls.

'Good morning, Mr Prentice. Did you sleep well?'

'Not too bad, chap. Have you recovered from last night?'

'Yes, just did what had to be done.'

'Is the young lass..'

'Nurse Phillips?'

'Yes, is she, you know, gonna be OK?'

'Well she's in good hands. If you're going to pass out, a hospital's probably the best place to do it.'

'And the baby?'

'No reason to think it won't be fine. Now who's for a cup of tea?'

'I think the Nurse...'

'No she'll be too busy. There's a new lot of fellas to prep this morning. Just one sugar wasn't it Mr Prentice – and you Mr Cornish?'

'Yes please.' Mr Cornish was improving by the minute, 'One sugar, please'.

Mick went over to Pauline who was completing Mr Cornish's transfer paperwork. 'Would you like a cup of tea Nurse, 'he read her name badge, 'Felician'

'Call me Pauline. It's easier. So what happened here last night.'

'Oh – well Nikki- Nurse Phillips – had been on duty for over 12 hours and she had three patients to move before she could go. One just needed pushing in a chair to his car but his elderly wife wasn't up to it and Nikki couldn't do it. Apart from being pregnant it would have meant leaving the other two here unattended because I'd been moved to A&E for an hour because they assumed the day ward had closed at 6 like it was supposed to. There were no porters available and I think her phone conversation with admin sent her bp over the top.

Anyway, I was in A&E when they brought her in and apart from a bit of bruising the Doctor thinks she'll be OK. They're keeping her in for a couple of days just to monitor the blood pressure.'

'Well praise the Lord for that.'

'But I reckon you'd better get used to mens' day ward because I think you'll be with us for a while. I'll go and get that tea shall I.'

As Mick went into the little kitchen, Dr Khan came in. 'Good morning, nurse, how are my two this morning?'

'Mr Prentice says he is able to urinate normally and Mr Cornish is beginning to sit up and take an interest.'

'Good, good. Hello Mr Prentice. Nurse, here tells me your waterworks are getting back to normal'

'Yes, doctor, no problem today.'

'Right, then I'll tell nurse that you can be discharged. And how are you Mr Cornish?'

'Well, I'm still a bit groggy but I'm a lot better than when I first woke up.'

'Good, well let nurse know once you've been to the lavatory and we'll think about letting you go. But don't go wandering around by yourself. If you're feeling dizzy, we don't want you tumbling down, now do we. OK, bye now.

Nurse, I don't recognize you. Do you know the day ward discharge procedures?'

'I think so. I've just come down from geriatrics.'

'Oh that's fine. I thought perhaps you'd just come in from an agency as a temporary replacement. In that case standard discharge for Mr Prentice – as soon as possible as I have four on my morning list so we need the beds. We'll give Mr Cornish a bit longer. I'll see how he is after lunch and again if he's still here at the end of the afternoon. Thank you for taking over the ward so smoothly.' And he was gone.

'Here's your tea, Pauline.' Mick was back.'

'Right, Mr Prentice. Doctor says you can get dressed and go home. Is there someone to ring to collect you?'

'There's Roger, my son. I said I'd ring him when I was ready..'

'OK, if you ring him now, do you need a phone? Tell him to park and come in and then I'll arrange someone to take you to the car in a chair.'

'I think I can walk to the car.'

'I think I am the nurse, and I say you go in a chair. This is my ward now, savvy?'

'Savvy, Nurse'. Pauline drew the curtains around the bed.

Mick liked this new nurse. 'When the time comes, do you want me to do it?'

'When the time comes. Now would you like to see if Mr Cornish needs accompanying to the lavatory? And thank you for the tea.' She started the drugs check singing to herself. She knew she had less than an hour before the first of Mr Khan's new patients would be in.

'You've got a lovely voice, nurse.' It was Mr Prentice from behind the screen. Do you sing in a choir?'

'Only at my church. The Pentecostal one on Bright Street. But I don't suppose you know that area.'

''Fraid not'.

'And if I can get off duty on time, there's a new choir starting tomorrow near where I live. I'm thinking I might go to that. Depends if we have more troublesome patients like you and Mr Cornish. How's the dressing going?'

'Well I'm decent now but I can't bend to do my socks.'

'Right, well, phone your son, then when Mick gets back he'll give you a hand'.

Pauline felt sorry for Nurse Phillips and hoped she was OK but it had given her the opportunity to have a ward of her own. Tonight she would pray for Nurse Phillips and her baby. And tomorrow if she got a lunch break, she thought she might just go and visit her.

Chapter 11 : Jason's exam

Jason had done better in his first year exams than he'd expected, so he had approached the new term with confidence. He decided to go and buy groceries and then sit and read in the cemetery which would be more peaceful early on a Sunday morning than his cramped room in a shared student house. It was one of those early autumn days when you knew winter was waiting in the wings ready for its cue but summer was still hanging on the stage enjoying its last moments of glory. Jason knew he had several chapters on Roman Britain to read that weekend and, seeing an empty bench, he decided to settle here. He put the carrier bag with the ingredients for his evening meal by his feet and his back pack on the bench beside him, took out Wembley's History of Northern England and started to read.

It was here that Sara first saw him. He was deep in Roman Chester at the time so was not really aware of her sitting down at the other end of the bench. He didn't notice when she produced a plastic bag from which she took a handful of birdseed which she sprinkled on the ground around her. He didn't see the second, which landed closer to him.

Her third handful accidentally caught his shoes and the bottom of his jeans. 'I'm so sorry,' she apologised. He came back to the twenty first century with a jolt.

For light relief he often read PG Wodehouse and now he wondered how long this vision of loveliness had been there. He noticed at once her azure eyes, her ruby lips her shell like ears and her pearl skin. Well he might have done if he'd been in a Berty Wooster novel. In reality he noticed her Glastonbury T shirt. And instead of falling at her feet and swearing undying love, he purely muttered ' 'salright.'

'I didn't mean to disturb you.'

Again, Berty Wooster would have heard the tinkle of tiny bells in her voice. Jason heard the trace of a Birmingham accent.

'It's obviously interesting. You were miles away.'

'I was actually, Chester, in AD 100.'

'Oh, I once went to Chester. They've got some lovely shops.'

'And have you been to Glastonbury?' he asked.

'What? Oh the shirt. Yes Twice. Have you?'

'No, well not for the music.'

'So are you a student?'

'Yes.'

'Of?'

'Ancient history. And you?'

'Me, no. I work in a shoe shop. And I do a bit of folk singing. Just locally. Not professional.'

'Really. I like folk music. Perhaps I could come and hear you some time. Have you any gigs coming up?'

'Not at the moment. If you give me your number I can let you know.'

Jason took out his phone and looked disappointed. 'Sorry, flat battery.'

Hang on,' she searched in her coat pocket for first a pen and then paper. She pulled out a brightly coloured flyer. He could see it was for something musical with a date on it as she wrote on the back'.

'Is that a poster for one of your gigs?'

'This, no this is a leaflet for a new choir that's starting up. I was thinking of going but I probably won't bother. Look this is my phone number. Ring me next week and I'll let you know if I've sorted any more gigs. Or we could just arrange to go to a folk club somewhere and see what's on'.

'That would be nice,' he said.

'Or just for a drink. Right then, see you.'

And she was up and gone. Jason sat for a moment then opened his book and tried to return to ancient Chester but he'd lost the thread. And he realised he was getting hungry. He returned the book to his back pack and picked up the carrier. A pack of potatoes, four apples, an onion and some carrots ripped their way out of the bag and settled amongst the bird seed. He picked them up and stuffed them individually into his back pack. The torn carrier went into his pocket and he set off to his temporary home. Meanwhile the breeze noticed the leaflet with the all important phone number, lying forgotten on the bench, picked it up and wrapped it around a memorial for the late Robert Winston, husband of Valerie.

Jason was still thinking about the girl as he unpacked his groceries. He realised that they had not even exchanged names. Still he had the – he checked his bag and his pockets – he hadn't. He must have dropped the phone number. Well, was he interested enough to visit every shoe shop? A bit Prince Charmingish he thought. Or perhaps he could visit folk clubs. Or perhaps they were just what his mum called ships that pass in the night.

By the time he had prepared his vegetable stew and put it in the slow cooker and begun an essay on the structure of the Roman army he had almost forgotten the encounter.

Sara went to bed that hoping he would call.

Chapter 12 : Phoebe's script

Auditions are terrible things. Phoebe knew that. It was worse than stage fright. You had such a short time to make an impact on whoever was doing the casting. She yawned. She was becoming bored and frustrated.

When Phoebe was asked what she was she would always reply that she was an actor. In fact, so far she had landed just one professional part, in a touring pantomime in the Manchester area. Not enough to get her an agent or into Spotlight.

She had wanted to be an actor for as long as she could remember. And she had put in the effort; drama college, various classes, getting head shots, a showreel. And so far. One pantomime. One provincial pantomime. One not very good provincial pantomime.

She remembered the arguments with her parents, particularly her dad, when she'd declared she was going to be an actress. Eventually he had supported her providing she had learned what he termed 'a trade' as well. So she had trained as a hairstylist for a year and then used those skills to pay her way through drama school. Last time she'd seen her dad she had thanked him for insisting.

One of the things she hated was whenever she went to visit her family there were the inevitable questions. 'When are we going to see you in Corrie?' 'Have you thought about auditioning for the new James Bond?' I'm sure if you spoke to Judi Dench / Martin Shaw / Sean Bean they'd be able to put you in touch.' 'I hear there's good money in adverts.' Adverts? They might as well suggest she took up modelling. OK she could probably do an advert for Weight-watchers or some such. She didn't think of herself as fat, more plumpish. Her dad said the modern word was curvy. Mind you he also described her as a hairdresser or, when the mood was on him, a women's barber.

At the moment she was working as a stylist in a salon on Market Street. It suited her. The wage was liveable and the set up flexible enough for her to go off to auditions when she needed to. Like today, when she'd been up for Macbeth. Literally. An all woman cast in which she was to double the King, Banquo and one of Macduff's sons. Except, of course, she wasn't because she hadn't got the part.

Apparently she wasn't tall enough. For heaven's sake, her height was on her CV. Why waste her time, not to mention her travelling expenses when they could see from her CV she was 5 ft 1in?

A fortnight ago, a Streetcar Named Desire had turned her down because her American accent wasn't southern enough.

She hadn't even got an audition for Heda Gabler because she 'couldn't play the bassoon.' What on earth was all that about?

Oklahoma said she hadn't got an ensemble singing voice and a new play, a nice little two character comedy aiming for the fringe had turned her down in favour of the playwright's wife.

The playwright was cast to play the other part. She could see that it was cheaper like that – and they would only need one room in Edinburgh.

She had considered putting together a one woman show to take to the Fringe herself. The trouble with that was so often one woman show's drew one woman audiences. And she knew that the chances on 'being discovered' by such a route were pretty thin.

Oh she was forgetting. She had been offered a part, no not just a part, the leading part, in a new play in a pub theatre in Lincoln. It was profit share and was entitled 'Humiliation'. The whole of the second act was to be played in the nude. She wondered if they'd ever managed to cast the role. Four actors, a techy and a director in a theatre that seated thirty-six. Profit share! Were they charging sixty pounds a seat?

Then there were the student horror films. Why did students have this affinity with zombies. And as they could never afford to pay, why didn't they get students from their own drama departments instead of expecting professional, trained actors like herself to do it 'for the exposure'. She didn't need their exposure any more than she wanted the Lincoln variety.

Anyway, back to the here and now.

'Would you like tea or coffee while you're under the drier, Mrs Widdowson,' she said, smiling at her client as she put her under the machine.

Chapter 13 : Bill's Jotter

Anybody who went into local politics was mad, Bill told himself as he put his jacket on and checked he had his keys, phone and wallet. Originally he had done it to try and improve his local community. He'd been younger then; with hair; and thin. But the whole structure of local government with its endless committees, interminable sub-committees and never-ending red tape meant that most initiatives ground to a halt long before they saw the light of day in any practical action.

He had now been a local councillor for 32 years. He was deputy mayor which meant that later in the year he would become mayor. He wondered whether he would bother to seek re-election after that. At least he had no meetings tonight and he was on top of his paperwork. Tonight he was going to go for a walk. He wanted to check the pot holes in Vine Street and examine how well the park gates had been repainted after their altercation with a delivery van. He could also check up on the state of the bowling green, and how it was surviving now that they'd cut the groundsman's hours. He tended to think bowling was big boy's marbles, but had the sense to realise some influential voters belonged to the club.

When he had first been elected as a councillor, his mother had seen it as the first step to being Prime Minister. She died a few years later without being disillusioned.

If he had time he would like to pop into the library to see how much the computer system was being used. He got regular reports from the manager but figures on a balance sheet were never as good as seeing anything with his own eyes.

Although he was no longer one of the school governors he

would pass the school. It would be too late to see if the local police had done anything about the parking or the drug dealing that was supposedly going on there, but he might run into a parent who could tell him something. Or, more likely, a teacher wending their weary way home.

He put his pad and pencil in his pocket. He used these to jot down street lights which were not working, blocked drains, graffiti and so on. His pad was well known not only in the council chamber but in every council office in the borough. If you were an officer of the council at any level and Bill Crowther got his pad out in front of you, you knew a problem was coming your way.

He would finish his walk at the Crown. He wasn't a great drinker but it was a useful place to meet potential voters and he'd heard that the pub was no longer the thriving business that it had been when he had first been elected. He was worried that this might be another local amenity to disappear. The swimming baths had gone a year ago, two of the five community centres had been closed and he wondered how much longer they would be able to keep the library.

He knew that the local postmaster was preparing for retirement and that the post office on Austerlitz Street would then be doomed to closure. The pub was on his mental list of possible replacement premises. It wouldn't be the first pub to double up as a post office. Apparently there was one up north which also hosted a monthly optician, an occasional MP's surgery, and a chiropodist, as well as the more traditional cricket and darts teams. And if The Crown couldn't or wouldn't do it, Bill couldn't imagine that the Polish shop or the Newsagents would have the space. Tomorrow he might go and see the manager at the supermarket.

Chapter 14 : Mr Turner's Newspapers

When Sophie was 11, her mother packed her bags and left the family home. Her dad talked about it as though it was a temporary thing, but Sophie knew it wasn't.

Some of her school friends said her mum had run off with the milkman. That was surprisingly close to the truth. Her mum had been tired of helping to run the ailing newsagents. To help make ends meet she had taken a job in the offices of the local manufacturing dairy where she had met Tony.

Tony had a nice car and a nice flat and took her on nice foreign holidays. Sophie had been taken to meet Tony and her mum had explained she was leaving and offered to take Sophie with her. But Sophie had said she didn't want to move away from her school friends. She also thought it was a bit mean if they both left and her dad was by himself. When she told them she intended to stay with her dad, she could see the relief on Tony's face.

Now she was about to become a teenager she decided it was time to make some changes. For nearly a year she had come home from school each day and immediately gone out to do a paper round. Then she'd prepared a meal for herself and her dad, nothing much usually. Then, by the time she'd done her homework it was time for bed. She knew her dad often stayed up very late watching TV and on a couple of occasions she had found him still sitting there the next morning. OK, he missed her mum but so did she.

Tonight she had put a frozen pie in the oven and accompanied it with frozen chips and frozen peas.

While they were eating she began to put forward her plan.

'Dad, I need your help.'

'To do what?'

'There's a new choir starting on Thursday evenings and I want to join.'

'That's OK by me. Will it get in the way of your homework.'

'No, but there is a problem.'

'What's that, love?'

'I need you to come with me.'

'Oh, I don't think so. I can't sing. No, you go and enjoy yourself. What time does it finish?'

'No, you don't understand. I have to go with a parent or they won't let me in because I'm not 16 yet.'

'Well I don't mind taking you and then coming home.'

'Dad, I don't like walking home by myself, in the dark'. This wasn't strictly true. She walked the same short route delivering the papers in the dark but she hoped her dad wouldn't notice.

'But I don't want to sing.'

'You could just sit and listen. Or read a book'.

He knew he wasn't going to win. She was just like her mother. She'd just go on and on until she got her own way. Or else she'd leave and join her mother.

'What day is it again?'

Sophie scented victory, 'Thursday, Dad.'

'Now do I get a cup of tea?'

She went into the kitchen. Get the choir thing going and then she'd work on getting him to make his own tea. She was his daughter, not his mother.

Chapter 15 : Stefan's Mail

Stefan looked proudly in the mirror. It was seven years since he'd arrived in this country looking for a new future. He thought back to Mr Giles, his first boss on the farm where he had been crop picking. There was obviously some joke about Mr Giles name but he didn't understand it. In those days he didn't understand much of the language. Just a few words – 'Fast', Hurry', 'Quick', 'OK'. But he enjoyed the work and sang Estonian folk songs to cheer up the workers at night. At the end of each week he would send a letter to his mother and father back home.

It had been OK. Mr Giles had paid what he promised and at the end of the season, when the rest of the workers had gone back to Estonia, Mr Giles had helped him with the official papers so he could move to the city and work on Mr Giles' brother-in-law's building site. That was OK too. Stefan liked working in the open air. He still sang his Estonian folk songs as he worked to the amusement of his work-mates. He still wrote his weekly newsletter home.

Then there had been the business with Mr Giles daughter. Nothing wrong, but Mr Giles wanted Stefan as a worker, not a son-in-law, so Stefan was given his wages and told not to come back to the building site.

But that was OK because the local council needed a sexton and he settled easily into that job. Occasionally the manager had to ask him not to sing at work because grieving families found it disturbing, but that was OK as well.

The council offered him a chance to go to English classes in the evening and, as he had nothing better to do he went. All the English people he had met had said how difficult his Estonian language was to learn. He didn't see how it could be harder than English (pronounced Inglish!). They had words that looked the same but were pronounced differently. You could 'lead a horse to water' but you were 'swinging the lead,' whatever that meant. And laughter was a good thing but slaughter wasn't. And they even had a town called Loughborough. How were you supposed to pronounce that. His teacher told him to say 'Luffbro' but he wasn't sure whether she was making fun of him.

But he enjoyed the classes. Sometimes the teacher taught them to sing English songs, children's songs like London's Burning and Old MacDonald had a farm. Emily, the teacher, told him he was her star pupil. And he learned about English traditions like cricket, and morris dancing and fish and chips. Though he wondered if this was another joke Emily was playing on them. His boss, Mr Paull, hated fish and chips and preferred curries and when he asked him about morris dancing he was told it was just a pile of eccentric loonies who used it as an excuse to get drunk. Mr Paull wasn't even interested in cricket but offered to take Stefan to the next home Fulham match.

Stefan didn't go to the match and when he asked Emily if she had been joking she said no but not all English people appreciated their heritage. Then she showed him a photo of her

70

in a morris group with a red painted face and a red and green costume, and explained there were all sorts of different styles and hers was a side for women and men and they were doing a display that Saturday if he would like to come and see it. He decided he wouldn't. But it was something interesting to write to his parents about.

One day, after class, he asked Emily about becoming a British Citizen and she promised to bring him some information.

Although she forgot the next week, the week after she remembered and helped him fill in the forms to start the application.

It was shortly after that when life changed again. Government cuts meant the council was removing jobs and the number of sextons was to be reduced. By one it turned out. And that one was Stefan. He would get a small amount of severance pay but that would be it.

Stefan didn't drink or smoke and had saved most of his earnings while he was in England so he wasn't immediately worried. On his last day Mr Paull came to bring him his documents and told him he was sorry to see him go because he had been an excellent worker. He gave him a slip of paper and said if he went to see a Mr George Craigleigh at that address there might be work and he, Mr Paull, would be happy to give him a reference. So that was OK.

And Mr Craigleigh said he would have three days training and then go out with a more experienced officer. But they were going to pay him while he was being trained so that was OK.

Yesterday he had been to the Civic Centre and sworn an oath. He was now a British Subject and could have a British passport.

Afterwards he'd gone straight to the bank to open a new account. First he'd given the lady his cheque from the council. That was all in order, she'd said, but he wouldn't be able to take any of the cash from it for about a week with it being a new account and everything. He told her that he had his savings from the last seven years so he would keep some for food and rent but put the rest into the account as well. She said that was OK but when he got the savings out she called the manager and he called the police. It seems in England it is unusual to have £32,000 in cash.

A very nice police lady and a police man came and they all went into a back office. It was very British. They all had a cup of tea while the lady police man borrowed his phone and checked with Mr Paull, Mr Giles, Mr Craigleigh and even Emily.

Then they all looked embarrassed and explained that usually the only people who carried large amounts of cash were criminals and they had to check every time people had that amount of cash and it was nothing to do with him being a foreigner. Which, of course, he wasn't. Not now. And the police wished him good luck in his new job and the bank said that his cards and cheque book would be posted to him and thanked him for choosing their bank. He would write and tell his parents about it all and how it all turned out OK.

Today he would sing at work, but not Estonian folk songs. He would sing Rule Britannia, and Land of Hope and Glory and Jerusalem, whatever that was all about. He had pronounced Mr Craigleigh's name correctly first time round, he had impressed them in the training period knowing the difference between ceiling and sealing and now he was standing in front of a mirror, a uniformed servant of Her Majesty Queen Elizabeth II of Britain.

He had mastered the English language with all its strange double meanings and, as his polished badge proclaimed, he was now a Royal Mail.

Chapter 16 Nigel's brief.

'Court number 6. The jury are returning. Court number 6. The jury are returning. '

Nigel heard the announcement, picked up his wig and put it on. He briskly left the robing room and took the stairs to court 6 two at a time.. It had been a straightforward mugging and Nigel had his speech in mitigation ready. Timmy Madison had been sent down before for similar offences and the evidence was pretty solid this time. Timmy had refused his offer to try and cut a deal – plead guilty for a lower tariff in effect. He insisted on his innocence despite it being clear that it was his MO and he matched the victim's admittedly sketchy description. He was a small, inoffensive looking man who would go up to his victim all sweetness and light. He would ask for directions to a place he knew was behind his victim and as she, and it was always a she, turned to point he would have a knife at her throat and be away with her handbag in seconds. That was exactly how Caroline Priest, today's victim, had been robbed.

Philip, the prosecuting counsel who was against him was

already in court along with both solicitors. The clerk had obviously been waiting for him because before he reached his seat she called 'All rise' and the court climbed to its feet for the entrance of Judge Simon. His honour was developing a reputation as a fairly harsh sentence giver. There was a story going the rounds that he carried a black cap in his case. When he came in he certainly looked as if he was about to, if not hang the miscreant, then at least have him transported.

'Right,' said his honour as everyone settled back into their seats, 'let's have the jury back'.

As the jury filed back in Nigel was surprised to see them each look at Timmy. It was common knowledge that a jury who were about to convict didn't look at the defendant.

The judge ran through the formalities, checking they had a foreman and had reached a unanimous verdict. Then he instructed the clerk to read out the charge which she did, followed by the time honoured, 'do you find the defendant guilty or not guilty?'

Not for the first time Nigel mused that it was an odd system of law where no-one was ever found 'innocent,' only 'not guilty.'

As if echoing his thoughts he heard the foreman of the jury say 'Not Guilty'. He was half way to his feet before the verdict registered with him.

'Mr Draper?'

Now he had to stand up, 'Nothing, your honour.'

'Ah, I thought you wished to say something?'

'No thank you, your honour.'

'Very well. Mr Madison you have heard the not guilty verdict of this jury and you are free to leave. Perhaps you and your solicitor would go with the usher as there will be some papers to sign.'

'All rise', the clerk knew not to keep his honour waiting. By the time Nigel was fully upright, the judge had gone.

Timmy and his solicitor came over and both shook his hand.

'There you are, said Timmy.' I kept telling you I was innocent.'

'Yes, you did,' Nigel replied. 'And the jury believed you'. If Timmy noticed the shift of emphasis, he didn't react to it. The solicitor led Timmy away and Nigel tied the red ribbons round the case file and reached for the next one. He'd read it the night before but wanted to refresh his memory.'

'So what happened there?' It was Philip, Timmy's prosecutor.

'Well they always say a jury trial is a bit of a lottery.'

'I know but I thought I'd put together a watertight case.'

'I thought so too. I was hoping for a late guilty plea, to be honest, to save the full trial, but there you go.'

'And I thought Sexy Blake had drawn a really good impact statement out of the victim.'

'She's going to hear you calling her that one of these days.'

'So? She knows everyone calls her that. I think she's quite flattered by it.'

'Mm. I don't even know her real name.'

'It's Susie.'

Nigel raised an eyebrow. 'You seem to know her better than me.'

Phillip smiled conspiratorially. 'You should take more prosecution work. Always good to keep the police on side.'

Nigel indicated his next bundle, 'I've got a Doreen Andrews next. Are you prosecuting?'

'No I'm in court 4 in 10 minutes. It's down as attempted murder but we'll see if we get a guilty offer on GBH. It's before Judge Plumtree so we might get it through fairly quickly.'

'Well excuse me, that must be my client just arrived with Jim Dickinson

'Fraud?' Philip liked to try and guess the charge from the appearance of the defendant.

'Arson. Are you still OK for squash on Wednesday night?'

'Oh no, sorry, I'm going out for dinner.'

'Would that be with Sexton Blake?.'

'Not necessarily'.

'Well offer her my condolences, Philip. I'll find something or someone else to do'.

Nigel turned and walked towards his client. 'Hello, Mrs Andrews, Mr Dickinson. Perhaps we can have a few words before the judge arrives.'

Chapter 17 : Susie's Pocket Book

PC 2104 Susan Blake checked her appearance in the shop window and then went into the station. The station sergeant was waiting for her.

'So how did it go this morning, Susie?'

'They acquitted him!'

Sergeant Oldman could hear the frustration in his officer's voice.

'Ah well, some you win, some you lose. So what went wrong?'

'I have no idea. Honestly, sarge, the CPS didn't think twice about prosecuting. He had no alibi, it was his MO all over it and the victim gave a passable description.'

'There'll have to be a report'.

'I know'. The voice sounded weary.

'Well as soon as you've written up your notes I've got a job for you.'

'Sarge?'

'Do you have any contacts at Brunswick High?'

'I don't think so'

'Well Councillor Crowther has been on at the super about somebody dealing drugs up there. They won't tell you much because of the uniform but you might get a couple of names for CID to look at.'

'I could always go in civvies'.

'You could not! I have to live with DI Underhand. If he found we were doing CID work... He's going to be bad enough when he hears Madison got off this morning. You can bet that'll be uniform's fault.'

'Yes, sorry, sarge. What about if I go up just before the school run? Doesn't the councillor also moan about the lousy parking?'

'Good idea. He does. But keep it low key. I don't want you filling your notebook with thousands of trivial traffic offences.'

'I know, sarge, sweetness and light'.

'But before that, write up this morning'.

'I'm on it.'

By mid afternoon Susie was outside the school. There were the usual crop of 4x4s parked half on the payment. Susie decided to work her way along the line so started with the one at the front of the queue. 'Hello there', big smile.

'I suppose you're here to moan about the parking.'

'No, but can I ask, do you think this is the safest place to park?'

'It is for me and our Anita'.

'But what about other traffic?

'What other traffic? I can't see any other traffic. Can you see any other traffic?'

'Not at the moment, but you are technically committing an offence'. She immediately regretted saying it. Sweetness and light, she told herself, sweetness and light'.

'Well why not forgot my technical offence and go and catch some real criminals.'

78

'Because my sergeant wants me to have a word with you guys. Of course, if you know of any what you call real criminals'. Now she had to raise her voice as a motorcycle started up and roared away.

'Well, as it happens, I do. My friend got mugged by a guy with a knife. She gave you police a description and today he walks out of court free. What about that then?'

'What I'm going to do is make a note of your vehicle registration number so that we can monitor your future parking'

'Right, you do that. Anita, over here darling.' A child almost as large as the mother climbed into the passenger seat. 'And I'll make a note of your registration number, PC2104 and monitor your policing. Anyway I'm off now so I won't be a problem for all this traffic any more.'

'Just doing my job, madam,' Susie said to a fast departing car exhaust. The driver of car number two was standing with his back leaning on the front passenger door of an old blue Mondeo, smoking a cigarette.

Big smile, 'Hello'.

'Are you the tobacco police?'

'Pardon?'

'Are you the tobacco police, like?'

'No?' Susie was puzzled.

'Because I'm not smoking in a car where a child is being carried'.

'Oh, I see. No. I was wondering if you could help me.' It was becoming harder to raise the big smile.

'I doubt it. Is this official, like.? Am I officially helping the police with their enquiries?'

'No, nothing like that, sir, it's just we've had reports of people dealing drugs around the school gates..'

'It's only tobacco. I don't do wacky backy or charlie or anything, like'

'I wasn't suggesting you were but I thought you might have noticed something out of the ordinary'.

'How do you mean, out of the ordinary, like?'

It was on days like this that Susie sometimes wondered if she was cut out to be a constable.

'Well, you know, something that makes you think, what's going on there? I didn't expect to see that.'

'Oh. No. Well there was one thing.'

'Yes'.

'There was a woman in a big 4x4 here a few minutes ago parked on the pavement and a copper came and talked to her and didn't even take her number when she drove off without a seatbelt.'

'Yes, OK, thank you for your observation.' She decided not to point out that she had already taken the 4x4's number before she started to speak to the driver, just as she had with him.

Susie spoke to seven or eight more parents without success and then went back to the station.

Sergeant Oldman had just got a mug of tea when he saw his youngest officer return

'How'd'ye get on?' he asked, 'Lots of grief from the parents?'

He wasn't expecting any real information but he had wanted to send an officer down to the school to keep Councillor Crowther happy and he needed to take Susie's mind off the perverse verdict of the morning.

'Not brilliant, but I did notice one thing. When I first got there, there was an ice-cream van parked outside the gate, but when it spotted me talking to drivers, it drove off.'

'Perhaps he'd sold out'.

'This was before the kids came out. Why park there with an empty van?'

'OK. That might be a possible lead. But to be honest,. So many TV shows have used that as a plot I think our real pushers would probably avoid it like the plague. Still, if you can remember the brand we can pass it on to criminal intelligence.' He felt the need to be positive and encouraging.

Susie shook her head.

'No. Well never mind.'

'On the other hand, I did get the vehicle registration number'...

'Did you now? You'll make sergeant yet. Do you know how to pass it to Criminal Intelligence?'

'I think so, Sarge.'

'Well go on, then'. He took a sip of his tea.

'There's one other thing. One of the drivers I spoke to drove off without putting her seat belt on. And I have her number as well.'

'Of course you have. Now what did I say about filling your pocket book?'

'Are you saying there are some laws we don't get to enforce, then, Sarge?'

He took a larger sip of his tea. It was on days like this that Sergeant Oldman sometimes wondered if he was cut out to be a Sergeant.

'No, I'm not saying that. When you've dealt with the ice-cream van you can check this woman on the PNC and send her one of our nice little leaflets explaining about the dangers of driving without a seat belt. And then it will probably be time for you to go off shift. Tomorrow I'm sending you out with Nick in the area car so don't drink too much tonight.'

'Sarge, you know I don't drink. That's not the right image for a police officer, even off duty.'

On the contrary, Sergeant Oldman was beginning to feel it might be the right image for him, even while still on duty. He took another mouthful of tea, swallowed it and started on a topic which had been in his mind for some days. 'Susie, speaking of image, are you aware that other people on the force have – well – a nickname for you.' He was at his most avuncular.

'You mean Sexton Blake, sometimes shortened to Sexy Blake?'

'Yes. Do you really think that's the right image for a police officer?'

'I think it's just a bit of banter. I don't feel threatened by it. It's no worse than you calling DI Underhill, DI Underhand or DI Underpants. '

'That's a bit different. He doesn't know I call him that.'

'I think you'll find he does, sarge. That's why he refers to you as Sergeant Too Old Man.'

Sergeant Oldman wasn't ready for this response and a lot of the goodwill he had felt towards the constable evaporated. 'Constable, I think this conversation is closed. Now go and finish your paperwork and then go and do whatever it is you do in the evenings.'

'Well sarge, most nights I've been studying for my sergeant's exams; now they're over I noticed a leaflet about a new choir starting up next week. I thought if I joined that, it would be a good way of keeping a profile in the community'.

'I didn't know you could sing.'

'I can't but the leaflet said that didn't matter'.

'Blake, you never cease to amaze me. If by any chance this choir ever gets to give a performance with you in it, please get me a ticket.'

'I shall hold you to that, sir'

Chapter 18 Molly's CV

Duncan was late into the office again today. He knew Annie could cope but it wasn't fair to rely so much on his PA. He dashed up the steps and through reception, swiping his card through the security lock and waving a quick greeting to Miranda behind the desk. He ran up the stairs to his first floor office.

As he opened the door he realised his visitors were already here.

'Ah here's Mr Fitzgerald now,' said Annie, 'Bang on time to show you our latest range.' She took his jacket and briefcase as he sat down. He noticed that not only had the visitors been served with coffee and biscuits but they also had the drafts of the new catalogue in front of them.

Hilary and Edward stayed with him for over two hours. They had a chain of 27 jewellery shops so counted as a medium customer for the firm. Last season they had ordered 30 lines from them and he hoped to sell them more for next. Despite the economic downturn, people still seemed to invest in jewellery. And Mystère d'Or sold some very nice lines.

When they left he had orders for nineteen new lines and retained sixteen. Seven of the new lines needed development.

Annie returned from escorting them to their car and together they started to sort the samples strewn over Duncan's desk. Those selected by the customers were tagged with quantities, price and what development, if any, was needed. Duncan had been doing this for a long time. He could look at a gold earring and work out where you could shave off a quarter of a gram of gold to make it lighter and therefore cheaper. When Annie had first joined the company she didn't know why he bothered but she had learned that if you were selling a thousand of each piece, these tiny quantities mounted up to substantial sums.

As they sorted the samples together she briefed him for the rest of the day. A new designer who was coming for interview at 12 was already waiting in reception, another medium customer was due at three and she had seven or eight contracts for him to sign with far eastern suppliers.

Then she checked if he had made arrangements for lunch. As usual he hadn't so she arranged to bring him back a sandwich from the supermarket when she returned from lunch. They often joked about the fact that despite being CEO of a business with £30m annual turnover it was usually a supermarket sandwich lunch if he was in the office or a burger and chips one if he was out visiting the bigger customers.

They finished sorting the samples and Annie took them out to her office and returned with a folder of contracts to sign and a tall girl who might easily have been a model but was in fact the prospective designer. Working with jewellery, Duncan was used to appraising beauty. He could instantly see her adorning the design office where he spent most of his time when not seeing customers. She might even be interested in the sales side of things. Annie was already finding out if she would like coffee and offering to take her coat. Damn, he'd missed her name. He glanced at the folders Annie had given him. Well done, Annie, the girl's application and CV where in the top one. Molly Gallacher.

Once she'd delivered the coffee Annie settled at her desk with the samples. She wondered if her boss would ever find the right woman for his personal life. He was late forties, with 'distinguished' grey hair. She knew he went to the gym every morning and it showed in his excellent physique. She knew Miranda in reception carried a candle for him but she suspected he would never mix business with pleasure. There had been rumours about a customer called Rosy but that was before her time and she knew nothing about it.

Her mind turned back to the samples. She dealt with the development ones first, emailing each of the manufacturers. From time to time her phone rang and at one o'clock she went for lunch.

When she got back there was a note on her desk telling her to please put the sandwich in the fridge as he had taken Molly out to lunch. She put his sandwich along with her own shopping in the fridge in her office.

She carried on creating the specification sheets for the items selected that morning, weight, stone quality size and cut and so on.

Just before three Derek arrived. He had been one of the first customers that Mystère d'Or had attracted and he was still part of their core business. He had a young man with him who was being trained to take over his business. He was introduced as Andi. Annie knew the rumours that he was Derek's love child but wasn't really interested. Whilst Annie professionally shared all her customers interests being able to converse happily on demand about association football, ornithology, dress making or model railways, she was genuinely enthusiastic about Derek's hobby. He sang with the Phil and she and her partner had been to some of their concerts. Some of the stuff she thought was a bit highbrow but much of it she really enjoyed.

For this visit she had some news for Derek. While she was

getting him and Andi coffee and spreading out the latest catalogues she chatted to them, telling them that she and her partner were about to join a choir near where they lived. Derek asked what the repertoire was like but she confessed she didn't know but was going to try it for three weeks as it was free. Derek said that the Phil was doing Belshazzer's Feast this season. He told her that he would have loved to sing the baritone solo but they got professional soloists and an orchestra for all their concerts. He gave her his rendition of the unaccompanied baritone first entry. In the midst of this Duncan arrived back from lunch. Annie made him a black coffee without being asked.

At 4-30 Duncan, Derek and Andi were still deep in conversation. She closed down her computer and collected her groceries from the fridge. She noticed the sandwich so left a note on her desk saying 'Your Supper is in the fridge'.

When she got home, Molly was already there cooking pasta.

'Well?' Annie asked.

'Very,' said Molly.

'And?'

'He offered me the job.'

'There, I told you.'

'But I'm not accepting until you tell him about the two of us. You know I don't think he even knows you're gay. He certainly doesn't think I am.'

'Did he...?'

'No. not at all, he was the perfect gentleman.'

Annie could imagine the lunch time picture. She remembered

her interview when Duncan had taken her to lunch. Perfect gentleman summed it up, courteous and entertaining. That had been four and a half years ago. And she still felt she barely knew him. She knew he had a large house about twelve miles from the office and that he liked expensive cars and fine wines because she occasionally had to book a car in for service or order wine for him, but otherwise he was a closed book.

'Why should he know about me? We just work together. I know very little about him. But I suppose you're right.'

Molly waited patiently.

'OK, tomorrow morning. I don't suppose he'll bother about us being gay, but I will find a way to tell him. Now let's eat and get ready for this choir. If we get there early there'll be time for a drink.'

Meanwhile, Duncan was on his way home to the large house he shared with his husband, James.

Chapter 19 Miss Ferguson's index card

'No copies of Kes left, and you call yourself a librarian!'

No she didn't. She called herself what she really was. Librarians were much higher up the food chain than she was. So far up it that her little branch didn't boast one. It didn't even have an Assistant Librarian. It had doddery Mr Spooner, the chief library assistant, and Dot Parker, the deputy chief library assistant and Michael, the library assistants' manager and at the bottom of the pile her and three others, the part-time library assistants. There used to be a librarian, but he'd gone two years before she arrived. A victim of government cuts. Everybody reckoned that if Mr Spooner did finally retire he wouldn't be replaced. They'd just drop the deputy from Dot Parker's title. There was already talk of losing one of the library assistants.

The girl in partial school uniform was still there.

'I'm sorry?'

'How am I ever going to get my GCSEs if I can't read the bleeding set book.'

'I'm sorry, I can't produce a copy out of thin air if I haven't got one, can I?' She realized as she was speaking that that was the only way she really could produce one. If she'd got one it wouldn't be out of thin air, would it. She'd just produce it from wherever it was. Oh dear, her mind was wandering. The figure at the other side of the counter was still speaking.

'You 'ad one for that slag, Colette Milner.'

'I'm sorry, you can't use that kind of language in here.'

'Well what would you call her?'

89

'I'll tell you what, if we fill in this card, when a copy of Kes comes in I'll let you know'. What's your name?' As usual the pen box on the reception desk was empty. How fortunate she always carried a pencil in her cardigan pocket for just such occasions.

"Ermione Smyth. That's Ermione with an aitch and Smyth with a Y'

'Y'.

'Because that's how it's spelt. S-M-Y-T-H'

'Yes, I know – and do you have an e-mail address?'

'Yes'

There was a pause. 'So what is it?'

'What you want to know for?'

So I can let you know'.

'Oh', the figure thought about this for a little while. ' – well it's 'Ermione dot <u>Smyth3@brunhighschl.com</u>. I think the 3's because there were another two 'Ermione Smyths already.

'Surely there's not another like you?'

'That's funny, that's what me mam said. She said....'

'And the book you want to order is Kes by ?'

"By Friday. Then I can read it at the weekend.'

'No, the author. Who wrote it?'

'How should I know. You're the bleedin' librarian.'

'Barry Hines.'

'Right. So if you already know, what you askin' me for?'

'I'll send you an email as soon as a copy comes back in.'

'Right, see you, Miss Ferguson' And she was gone.

Miss Ferguson tried to look on the bright side. At least Hermione could read. Miss Ferguson was the name on her badge. All the staff had to wear name badges. Except for Mr Spooner, because of his seniority. And Miss Parker because she was his deputy. And managers didn't wear them so that let Michael off. And, come to think of it, Carmen, the cleaner didn't have to wear one because in theory she didn't have any contact with the public. In practice, if the public dirtied her toilets or trod mud into the carpets, they often came into contact with her, usually clutching a broom and with a menace in her voice which suggested her broom might imminently also come painfully into contact with them.

Now she thought of it, she realised that she hadn't noticed the other three assistants wearing theirs recently.

She looked at Hermione's card and thought of simply binning it, but that was not library policy. She would check on the computer in a moment. First, while there were no other clients in, she would tidy the notice board. Nobody else thought to remove out of date adverts for concerts, badly graffitied posters and unauthorised and often inappropriate adverts that the clients would put up when her or her colleagues' backs were turned. As she crossed the entrance area she wondered if graffitied was really a word.

Sure enough she found a plumber's card and one for an electrician. This was the Brunswick Street Library, not B&Q. Then she saw the one advertising a job in the library service. Halfway through reading it , at the point where the 'personal qualities ' had started to include 'no sense of humour and a lot

91

of attitude with a liking for drab clothing and cardigans' she realised it must be a joke. She didn't really see what the joke was, but clearly the library service would not really advertise for such a person. Underneath was a leaflet with the word Free written in large letters three times on the cover. It was for a new choir starting in the pub just up the road on Thursday evening. The poster was a bit gaudy by her standards but it suggested that they would be singing everything from Bach to Billy Joel.'

She remembered her school days when she had sung in the choir. They had made a CD of Bach's 'Jesu Joy of Man's Desiring' which had been sold to parents. It had been played on local radio a couple of times. She'd enjoyed that. Perhaps she'd give this new choir a go. Even if it did meet over a public house. What was it that Michael said, ' It was good to get out of your comfort zone from time to time.'

She put the poster in her handbag and logged on to the computer. She'd been happy with the old card index system but she had to admit, this was quite efficient.

She typed in Hines, Kes and was informed that her branch had two copies, one out on loan, and elsewhere the borough owned seven copies. That meant there should be a copy in her library somewhere so she set off to Fiction, Ha – Ho.

Craig Madison, youngest and brightest of the Madison family took this opportunity to access the unattended and logged on computer. It was the work of seconds to effect some changes to the entire system. He had subsequently disappeared as quietly as he had arrived.

Eventually the unsuspecting Miss Ferguson arrived back at reception clutching the copy of Kes to find an irate Michael standing there.

'Can I help you, Michael?' she said.

'Where have you been?'

'I was just finding this for one of our clients.'

''Did you leave your computer logged on and unattended?'

'Yes. But I thought I would only be away for a moment.'

'I see.' Michael's tone was distinctly hostile.

'Has something happened?'

'Could you find me, on the computer, a well-known title by the author Lewis Carol?'

'I don't need the computer..'

'On the computer, please.'

She typed in 'Lewis Carol' and was rewarded with an answer. 'There you are, Michael, Alice in Wonderland.'

'I think you need to read it again, Miss Ferguson.'

'Alice in – Oh my goodness.'

'Yes, Oh My Goodness, indeed, Miss Ferguson. Alice in Wankerland. And every single occurrence of the word wonder has suffered the same fate, from the biography of Stevie Wonder to the history of Wonderwoman. I won't waste time asking you to look up Footballing Tips for Boys. I can tell you that not only has Footballing been replaced by another word beginning with f, but tips has had its p changed to a t.'

'Perhaps it's a virus?'

'Yes, perhaps, but I think it's more likely to be that nuisance,

Craig Madison. He was hanging around earlier looking for mischief'.

Michael was right. Craig Madison had used the time whilst Miss Ferguson was looking for 'Kes' to select six words and ask the computer to exchange them for six different words where-ever they occurred. The six words removed were harmless adjectives. The six replacements had not so long ago been banned from the stage by the Lord Chancellor.

'Michael, I'm so sorry. What can I do?'

'Haven't you done enough? This is why we have rules requiring us to log off whenever we leave the keyboard. Fortunately I've programmed it to back up every thirty minutes so we can revert to that. But can you imagine if Mr Gregg from the borough had come in and checked. Or Deputy Mayor Crowther. It would reflect badly on the entire staff.'

Miss Ferguson was close to tears. 'I understand that, Michael.'

'Good,' he said and turned on his heel.

Miss Ferguson blew her nose and went over to the accursed computer. She opened her email account, typed in Hermione Smyth's address and sent her a message that Kes was now available to collect.

She carefully logged off and looked up to see the cherubic face of a small boy looking at her over the counter..

'Excuse me miss, but do you have a book called 'Footballing Tips for Boys?' said Craig Madison with an angelic smile.

94

Chapter 20 : Tim's memorial

When Tim Dalby was 5 he was the tallest boy in his class. At ten he was the tallest person in the school and apart from the caretaker, the heaviest. And after a number of nicknames including 'Obelisk' and 'Danny' a reference to Daniel Lambert, the world settled on calling him by the obvious soubriquet 'Tiny Tim.' Although he was big, he wasn't fat, and although he loved sport, he was never very good at it. At 15 he looked like a rugby player, but his inability to change direction at any kind of speed proved embarrassing on a number of occasions. There were Russian shot-putters who were smaller than him, but he lacked their sense of direction. He enjoyed swimming but not competitively in public where spectators compared him unflatteringly to a beached whale.

Whilst not academically gifted, he was by no means unintelligent. He enjoyed art in a free expression kind of way and made a passable noise on a tuba in the school band. He had a slight talent for gardening and immense patience but careers advisors were beginning to despair.

And then one sunny afternoon he missed the school bus to a theatre trip so reported to Mr Thicket, the art teacher, who improvised by giving Tim some protective glasses, a block of sand stone, a mallet and a small chisel and sending him outside to make a 'small statue based on nature'. Mr Thicket had forgotten him when at 5.30 after all the other students had left and he was putting his coat on Tim brought him back the tools and a small, but beautifully proportioned rabbit.

Mr Thicket's first reaction was to ask what had happened to the rest of the stone, as visions of Tim reducing the whole block to dust with just this rabbit to show for it flashed before his eyes.

But before he could comment, Tim asked Mr Thicket to come outside. He led him to the corner of the school building and pointed to a spot about 20 inches from the ground. There on a weather worn stone he could just make out the legend 'This stone was laid by Alderman Joshua Edwards, 4th June MCMXXVI.'

'I thought it was a shame it was so badly worn,' said Tim, 'so I made a new one, sir'.

And there on the floor was a pristine, sandstone perfect copy in neat Roman script.

Mr Thicket stood for a moment and said,' Tim, that's – that's – professional. I don't know how we could remove the old one to replace it with this, I think that's a question for the headmaster, but, Tim, you are a born craftsman'.

Tim wasn't actually sure if he was being praised or not but the following day Mr Greer, the career's advisor sent for him and asked if he would be interested in an apprenticeship with a stone mason. After a meeting with his mum and a Mr Jolley who was, it turned out, the local monumental mason it was agreed that Tim would go to work for Mr Jolley and learn the craft.. Whilst Tim was by now 6ft 4 tall and broad shouldered, Mr Jolley was a wisp of a man with thinning grey hair and a straggly moustache.

The one thing they had in common was that neither were great conversationalists. On the first day of Tim's indenture they spoke no more than twenty sentences apiece. Most days they spoke less. On some days they didn't speak at all after the opening 'good morning'.

Mr Jolley had a huge collection of classical music CDs which he played as background music in the workshop and each day Tim became more acquainted with the music from Bach to Schoenberg. After a while he could be heard, singing along to Schubert's songs or the Verdi requiem.

The company was called Jolley and Son and Tim never quite understood that the original Jolley was dead and this Mr Jolley was, in fact, the son of the son in the title. And this Mr Jolley didn't have a son. He once mentioned he had had a daughter who had died in an accident but in the whole time Tim worked there it was only mentioned this once and no details were ever given.

But Mr Jolley took great care to ensure that Tim learned all the aspects of the business from sales to accounts even though Tim's interest was always first and foremost the carving. He once asked Mr Jolley if he could have the off-cuts of the stones to take home and work on in his spare time and as the years passed he created an increasing number of carved miniatures of his own which adorned the Dalby house. Tim soon learnt to get the best from each different material, soapstone, marble, slate.

When Tim was 19 Mr Jolley arranged for him to have driving lessons. He said that this was so that he could help with deliveries. But once Tim had passed his test Mr Jolley took him out and helped him buy a car. He said it was a reward for three years hard work. By now, most of the locals referred to Tim as 'Jolley's Lad'

On his 23rd birthday, Mr Jolley told him his apprenticeship was finished and offered him a junior partnership in the firm.

A year after that, Mr Jolley had a slight stroke and from then on he took less and less part in the business.

Shortly after that, Tim's mother suddenly died. She had been carrying a malignant tumour but had neglected to complain to the doctor about it. Tim set about carving her memorial.

As a partner, Tim thought that perhaps he ought to do something to develop the business so one day he brought back some of the little statues he had made at home and put them on display. On the first day a man came in, pointed at a small marble statue and said,' Did you carve that?' When Tim nodded the man said, 'How much?'

Tim was used to pricing up gravestones but hadn't thought about the squirrel. 'Well it's marble' he said, thinking out loud.

'£500,' said the man. 'That's my final offer'.

Tim realised he might have been apprenticed in the wrong business if one squirrel brought as much as half a gravestone. He took the £500. He sold two more statues that afternoon as well as taking two orders for gravestones.

He was about to finish and lock up when two young women came in. It turned out they just wanted him to display a leaflet for a new choir they were starting at the pub. They asked him about the music playing in the workshop and he told them about Mr Jolley's CDs. Because they'd delayed him, he was still there when the man from earlier came back and gave him a business card and a proposition. That night Tim did something he had never done before. He went to Mr Jolley's house.

The following morning an elderly Mr Thicket at Brunswick High received an unexpected visitor. Despite the passage of years Mr Thicket recognised Tim at once.

'Well Mr Dalby, I gather you've done alright for yourself.'

'Reckon. So I've brought you a small present, sir. For you and,

I don't know if you have a wife.' He handed over a box. 'do you remember this, sir?'

'I certainly do. It's that rabbit you carved here.'

'Yeh. Well as it's the first piece I ever done and you know what, I think it might be valuable one day. It seems I'm to have an exhibition.'

'Really?'

'Yes, sir. This art dealer came in and bought a couple of my pieces. So I thought, it's all down to Mr Thicket so I thought I would bring you this.'

'Well done. Thank you, Tim, I shall treasure it'.

'And you can do something for me, Sir, if you would?'

'And what's that? How can I help?'

'Well, what with the exhibition and Mr Jolley not being well, and everything, I wondered if you could look out for a lad who might want to be my apprentice.'

' I'll do my best but you know Tim you're one of a kind. I'm pleased things are going well for you. Just remember all work and no play makes Jack a dull boy.'

'Yeh, you used to say that when I was here. I'm still not sure what it means. But apart from the stone work. Mr Jolley taught me something else. He taught me about music. He always had music on in the workshop, not pop music and stuff but proper music. And there's a new choir starting up so I thought I might give it a go.'

'You do that, Tim. And well done. I'm proud of you.'

'Thank you, sir. In that case are you proud enough to come and give a little speech at the opening of my exhibition?'

'What, me? If I can, I'd love to. Look, here's my home address', he wrote on a piece of paper.' why don't you come to tea and we can discuss the details? Let's arrange a date now'.

Chapter 21 : Jenny's register.

'Build it and they will come.' thought Jenny. Well she was about to find out if they would. In a moment of optimism she had printed 50 copies of five pieces she hoped to work on at the first rehearsal. As she headed towards the pub she ran through what she would do as warm ups tonight. Tamsin would be there already setting up her keyboard.

She turned the corner and The Crown came into view. Oh damn. There were six or seven people standing outside. Sam had chosen tonight of all nights not to open up. She hoped he wasn't sick. But then she realised she could see the people were drinking. She went up to the first couple and asked if they'd come for the choir? When they said yes, she introduced herself and said she'd hoped for a few more.

A lady who she was later to know as June Ferguson said, 'There are more. Many more. We came outside because it was so very crowded.'

And by now Jenny could see that this was the truth. She struggled in and made her way to the bar. Behind it Sam and

Tamsin were both working to meet the demand for drinks..

'Who are all these people?' she asked.

Tamsin replied, 'This, Jenny, is your choir.'

Sam was more prosaic. ' Now you're here, perhaps we can get them upstairs. One of your lads, a big guy called Tim, helped me set out extra chairs so you should be OK.'

'Thanks, Sam. Er ladies and gentlemen...'. She clapped her hands and slowly quiet descended on the saloon bar. 'Ladies and gentlemen, if you would like to make your way upstairs we'll make a start.'.

Once everyone was seated upstairs she introduced herself and Tamsin. She started with a few simple physical exercises followed by some easy voice warm ups calling for the occasional note or chord from Tamsin. These were all well received so she moved on to part two.

'Right, I'm going to split you into four. Please don't move until I've finished speaking. If you are a lady with what you think is a high voice, I'd like you to sit over here. For the time being, you are sopranos. Ladies with low voices, you will be over here. Gentlemen with higher voices, you will be tenors and be over here. And, guess what, chaps with low voices you'll be over here. You'll be basses. And if you haven't a clue what you are, just sit with a friend and we'll sort you out later. OK I've finished.' There was a pause then it seemed everyone stood up and moved around the room. But within a few minutes everyone was seated again, some in a new place but many just moving a seat or two to give the appearance of purpose..

'OK, here's the first piece we're going to look at. Don't worry if you can't read music. Just pass the sheets out. I'm afraid you'll have to share. All our music will be Christmassy and we'll start with this – The Virgin Mary had a Baby Boy.'

She noticed the two black women smile at each other. It was a smile that indicated that they both knew and approved the choice.

And so rehearsals began.

June Ferguson liked the tight organisation. She knew all about shortages so sympathised that they had to share music. It was just like her library.

Carol, or Carl as he had decided to be known here, enjoyed the Latin of Gaudete. It reminded him of his Polish catholic upbringing.

Barbara liked the organisation of little tips. Nothing big and complicated but simple and effective.

How to be a good choir member, listen, listen and listen.

Listen to yourself. If the noise you are making is unpleasant we'll work on making it nicer.

Listen to the rest of the choir. No matter how beautiful you and they sound, if you are not together, it will sound dreadful.

And finally listen to how your voice blends in with the others. It should not be a choir with a hundred separate voices but a choir that sings with one. Blend, blend, blend.

Richard Carlston was among the first to recognise that this choir leader had a rare talent. Her intonation was as perfect as any singer he knew and ten minutes into the rehearsal it was clear that she could inspire this motley group. Perhaps she would like to start a choir in his school. One thing troubled him though. There was a soprano who kept turning and smiling in his direction. He felt he ought to know her but couldn't place her. That was not surprising. Out of uniform and heavily made up, Colette from 4b could easily have passed for 18.

One or two people arrived late but were quickly absorbed into the group. Sara noticed that one of them was her student of history, the boy she'd given her phone number to. That might be embarrassing as she was still waiting for his phone call.

On this first night they managed, eventually, a reasonable shot at the spiritual, a promising start to Gaudete, a fair bit of Silent Night, a look at the descant in O Come all Ye Faithful, and finished with the beginning of 'All I want for Christmas is my two front teeth'. Halfway through Jenny interrupted the rehearsal.

'Ladies and gentlemen, much as we are enjoying ourselves there are a few business matters to sort out.' She explained that after three weeks she and Tamsin would have to charge and needed a lump sum for the rest of term. She outlined her plans for a Christmas concert and finally she remembered to pass a sign up sheet round so that she had a name and contact number for everyone.

The rehearsal finished when Jenny noticed Tamsin tapping her watch and giving her a look. She realised she'd overrun by ten minutes. Nobody seemed to mind and everybody made their way back downstairs to the bar. Tamsin was packing her keyboard and Jenny was collecting music when they were aware of a huge man waiting for them.

'Thank you for tonight, miss' he said. 'do you want me to stack the chairs for you?'

'Is it Tim?' asked Jenny who remembered Sam's description.

103

When he nodded she thanked him but told him it wasn't necessary.

'But thank you for helping Sam to set up earlier.'

Tim smiled with pleasure and mumbled ' s'alright, miss' and then with surprising agility for a man of his size disappeared down the stairs.

Tamsin looked tired but satisfied. 'Happy with that, Jenny'

'Let's see how many we have on week four before we go overboard.'

'There are 98 names on the register'.

'There'll be less next week.'

As they walked down the stairs and into the bar, spontaneous applause broke out embarrassing both of them. Tired as they were, they stayed for nearly an hour socialising The guy with the stubble bought them both drinks and told Jenny he'd once been in a group. A middle aged lady told her about how she used to be a teacher. A younger man with an eastern European accent said how much he'd enjoyed it. Jenny noticed that Tamsin was talking to a younger woman with too much make up. There was an older guy talking to a middle aged lady with glasses. Jenny worked her way over to them.

'Hello,' lovely to see you both. Hope you enjoyed it. How did you hear about us?'

The lady explained she had seen a flyer in the library. She didn't mention she'd taken it down.'

The older man, who introduced himself as Bill Crowther said he'd just come in for a drink and when everybody had gone upstairs he'd followed them out of curiosity. Jenny asked if he would come again and he said he would like to but he often had meetings on a Thursday evening.

Little by little the pub emptied and when it was down to about a dozen, Jenny made her way to the bar.

'Was that OK, Sam?' she asked.

'I don't think OK does it justice,' smiled a happy Sam. ' Do you feel like running a choir every night of the week?'

Jenny laughed, 'Thursdays is enough.'

'Well it was a good job that your mate, Tamsin could help behind the bar when they first arrived. You told me 20 or 30 . For next week I've arranged with your Polish guy to come in at half six. He's worked a bar before so I'll pay him for a couple of hours to cover before and after. He was talking earlier about starting a Polish club here. Dominoes and the like. Not on Thursdays, of course.'

'That's very good of you, Sam, but it might drop to 20 or 30. there's no guarantee they'll be back next week. Or when we start to charge.'

'No problem.'

Chapter 22 : Valerie's pictures

Valerie had had a lovely evening.

On Sunday Mr Rossini had collected her from the church as promised and after visiting the cemetery they had gone for tea at the cafe. Valentino had admitted that he already knew her name was Valerie; he had seen it on Robert's memorial.

It was a different girl serving at the cafe this time but she obviously knew and liked him as a regular customer..

He had suggested they come to the choir together and they had walked side by side from her house.

The weather had been warm without being uncomfortable and they had arrived at the pub in enough time for him to buy them a glass of wine each. They had sat outside to enjoy it.

After the practice they had walked home together and she had invited him in for coffee. He had tactfully suggested that the phrase often carried overtones but coffee and a biscuit would be lovely.

She explained about Phoenix her rather timid rescue cat and hoped he wasn't allergic. In turn he told her about his elderly cat that had come from his wife's sister as a kitten.

They had sat and chatted until the early hours. First he admired her house and asked if the pictures were of Robert. When she said they were he said what a handsome man he had been. He showed her a picture of his Sylvia from his wallet.

They spent some time discussing the choir programme.

She thought the two front teeth song was a little childish but liked everything else they had done. Valentino liked the Latin one because it came from Italy.

He commented that she seemed to know a lot of the people there and she confessed she'd allowed herself to drift away from them since Robert died.

She admitted that it had been nice to see June Ferguson from the library again. In the old days when she'd taught English they'd occasionally gone for coffee together and once or twice to the theatre. She recognised the music teacher from the school where she had worked. Richard was his name. He used to be in a band and had started at the school about a year before she left. She was surprised he was still working there.

She told him about Bill Crowther and how he'd once been one of the school governors and was now deputy mayor.

Eventually she'd asked his advice. She explained that she had recognised one of the girls. Her name was Colette Milner and she remembered teaching her. She had worked out that now she was only 14 or 15. Apart from the rules of the choir, there was also the fact that they were in a pub. She wondered whether she should tell Jenny or perhaps the pub landlord. She was prepared for Valentino to tell her that it wasn't her problem and not to get involved. That's what Robert would have done. Instead Valentino thought carefully and then suggested a solution. Why didn't she have a quiet word with this Colette. If she was that keen to join the choir they could offer to take her as 'responsible adults'. Obviously they would have to speak to her parents to approve it. Then they could make sure she didn't infringe the landlord's licence.

Valerie suddenly realised how much she missed having anyone to discuss things with. Since Robert's death she had not only given up teaching but had avoided her friends. Most of them had also been Robert's friends too and she couldn't bear their constant sympathy mingled with embarrassment at not knowing what to say. Although she still attended morning service at St Peter's she no longer helped with the flowers or the Sunday school. Colin, the vicar had been given short shrift when he had attempted to visit her pastorally. And she had snubbed, Linda, her sister-in-law who she knew must have been grieving the loss of her brother. She began to sob and Valentino produced a handkerchief and passed it to her. He didn't seem embarrassed by it or anything, just sat there patiently. She blew her nose and said ,'I'm sorry about this.'

'No problem, came the charming Italian accent, 'I, too, weep for the loss of my wife.' They sat in silence for a while and Valerie lost all sense of time. Eventually, Valentino said, 'I think it is time to go now. Would you like me to collect you again from the church on Sunday?

'Yes please, that would be very nice and,' she paused, 'Thank you.'

'That's alright. And on Thursday we will sort out the ex-pupil'.

'Colette. Well we can try. I don't remember the family as being very supportive'

'It's a great pity you stopped teaching. I think you were probably very good and caring for your pupils.'

'I would like to think so. But I did, so that's an end to it.' She realised that Phoenix had at some point got himself on to Valentino's chair and was dozing with his head on Valentino's lap.

She stood up and gently picked up Phoenix. 'Just after 11 on

Sunday?'

'It will be my pleasure.'

It was only after he'd gone that she realised she still had his handkerchief.

'So are you comfortable with him?' she asked Phoenix, ' because I hope he's coming again.'

Chapter 23 : Choir emails

Jenny Lint: Hello choir. Thank you for working hard and making such a lovely sound last night.. I attach some practice files for the three pieces we worked on yesterday.

Next week I want to start on Peter Cornelius' three kings carol and I wondered if any of you chaps would like to have a go at the solo.

Also, we need a name for the choir. Any suggestions x Jenny

Richard Carlston: Hi Jenny, I wouldn't mind having a bash at the Cornelius. I'm the one who spoke to you afterwards about having been in a band.

CarolthePole: Hi Jenny. Some of our singers might not have computers. Shall I run off some CDs.

Jenny Lint: Hi Richard, thanx 4 the offer. We'll have a go on Thursday. I've attached a youtube link for you to have a listen to.

Jenny Lint: Hi Carl, good idea. Just do half a dozen to see how it goes.

June Ferguson: The Crown Singers.

Nigel Draper: The Coronary Singers :)

Richard Carlston: The Chronic Singers.

Molly Gallacher: Can we do actions to all I want for Christmas?

Barbara Prince: The Harmonies.

Richard Carlston:: The raging Harmonies :)

Molly Gallacher: What are we going to wear?

Pauline Felicion: The Crown ensemble.

Molly Gallacher: The Crown Jewels :)

Nigel Draper: The Thirsty Knights (it's when we meet)

Kim Brookes: The St Peter's Singers

CarolthePole: Concordiant

Zoe Palmer: The Crown Community Chorus

Jenny Lint: I forgot to mention that there'll be no practice on October 22nd as it's half term. See u all on Thurs x

Jenny Lint: Hi Tamsin. If the numbers do stay this large we won't get them into the side room at the church for a concert. Even without an audience.

Tamsin Brocklehurst: The main church would be OK if we could get some lighting in. Would that be OK with the vicar of doom?

Jenny Lint: OK let's wait and see. We don't need to decide till half term.

Richard Carlston: The school half term is October 15th

Jenny Lint: OK sorry. No practice on 15th for half term. Restart on October 22nd.

Chapter 24 : Mr Carlston's packet

Mr Carlston had had yet another bad day.

It had started innocuously enough with a first year class. He was teaching them about Tchaikovsky when he noticed one of the boys fiddling with a phone under the desk.

'You, boy, what's your name?'

'James, sir, James Proctor.'

'Phoning the girl friend, are we?' he asked the 11 year old. The class tittered.

James Proctor squirmed in embarrassment and blurted out, 'No Sir. You said Tchaikovsky wrote Peter and the Wolf and I was just checking on Wikipedia'.

'Were you,' said Mr Carlston, 'and Wikipedia says what?'

'Well the only Peter and the Wolf they've got is by Prokofiev.' James wasn't sure of the pronunciation. 'Is there another Peter and the Wolf, sir?'

The titter escalated to a giggle

Mr Carlston stood up and started down the aisle to confiscate the offending phone. 'Are you trying to be funny, lad?' And with perfect timing he fell over his briefcase.

During the ensuing uproar he climbed to his feet to discover Mr Thomas in the doorway.

'Everything alright Mr Carlston?'

'Yes, fine, thank you, headmaster. I tripped over my briefcase.'

' Perhaps you might like to consider the school health and safety policy before you place your briefcase in a gangway in future.' Mr Thomas could feel the suppressed amusement of the class. He had been teaching a long time and knew that the briefcase wasn't the whole of it. He spoke to the class, 'And I hope not to hear that sort of noise again from 1b. Is that understood. 'There was a mumbled, 'yes Sir'. He turned and opened the door to leave and without glancing back said, ' And James Proctor, I hope I didn't see a mobile phone under your desk when I came in.' The door closed, and he was gone.

The rest of the morning passed without incident apart from a memo coming round 'inviting' heads of department to a 'brief meeting' after school to discuss the forthcoming open day for the local primary schools to visit. Although he wasn't paid a head of department's allowance, as the only music teacher he was expected to be there. And he knew the head would mention starting a choir again. He really needed to get the Jenny person on board quickly.

He was only rostered to do lunch duty once a fortnight but today was the day. It wasn't usually onerous. It just involved sitting in the dining hall and sorting out any problems which arose. Brunswick wasn't a difficult school and the most dramatic event he could remember was a couple of years ago when a boy with a nut allergy had eaten a hazelnut whirl. Fortunately Frank Thicket had been on duty that day and sorted out the ambulance and calling the parents.

He collected his lunch from the counter and made for the only empty table. He fancied sausage and chips but the nanny state dictated he got quiche and lettuce. As he sat down he was joined by three year nine girls who he recognised. His stalkers. Just what he needed.

'Hello Mr Carlston,' said the monster he knew was Hermione. 'We've seen a youtube clip of your band today. Why were you called Shaggzz? Was it because of all the girls – well you know.' She simpered provocatively and pretended to look coy.

He had planned to stay silent but decided to nip the conversation in the bud. 'It was because of my long hair and beard, as you would have realised if you had looked at the pictures.'

'Oh, we did. Lots of times.' said the second girl whose name he had forgotten..

'Are you going to start a choir here?' said the third one. He remembered her name was Colette and he was about to answer when the scales fell from his eyes. It was the soprano from the front row of the Thursday night choir. The one who had kept turning round to look at him.

At that moment he hated these three girls more than he hated the judge who had said that motorcyclists who drove too fast and whom subsequent drug tests showed had used cocaine in the last twenty four hours were partly responsible for the injuries sustained when they ran into white vans emerging unexpectedly from side roads and then slashed his compensation as a result.

113

He turned his attention to the question. 'Possibly,' he said. 'I have a meeting after school today with the headmaster. On the subject of choirs, Colette, I noticed you on Thursday evening. I thought that choir was for adults, or at least those over 16.'

'It is, sir, unless you have a responsible adult with you.'

'And do you have a responsible adult?'

'Oo, are you offering, sir?'

'I'm afraid not. I keep school and my private life separate.'

At this point Miss Kendrick interrupted, ' Is this seat taken?'

'No,' said Mr Carleton, ' Please join me – us.'

'Hello, miss,' it was Hermione again,' Mr Carlston was just telling us that he keeps his school life separate from his private life.'

Mr Carlston had finished the quiche and couldn't face the salad. At that moment he would happily have bought everyone in the dining hall a hazelnut whirl in the hope of finding a child with a nut allergy.

'What brought that on?' asked Miss Kendrick.

'Mr Carlston belongs to the same choir as me,' said Colette.

Miss Kendrick looked at Mr Carlston and raised her eyebrows quizzically.

'It only started on Thursday and by chance we both went to the first rehearsal.'

'Mm, you didn't strike me as being the choral type, not with your background.'

'Well of course you don't know me, do you. If you'll excuse

me.' He stood up and took his tray back to the trolley point. Well at least he only had two hours teaching during the afternoon. And then the headmaster's meeting. He'd arranged to meet Matt by the school gates so he'd have to be quick. At last the bell rang to call the faithful to afternoon lessons.

At 3-30 when the bell went for the end of the day he was out of the front door of the school before most of the kids. Matt was leaning against his motorbike as usual. But Mr Carlston could see that the copper was back talking to parents about parking. He went over to Matt and hissed 'There's a copper'.

'I know. Don't worry. She can't see us because the ice-cream van's in the way. Cash?'

The money and packet were exchanged quickly.

'Same time next week?'

Mr Carlston's answer was drowned in the roar of the motorbike starting up and driving off, weaving between the clusters of kids.

In the event, Mr Thomas's meeting was finished by ten past four and while the choir had been mentioned it was obviously fairly low down the list of priorities. Certainly below the small issue of the school's health and safety policies.

By seven fifteen he had eaten a ready meal, was showered and changed and propping up the bar in the Crown. He wanted a quiet word with Jenny about the Cornelius solo which he really did know. He'd sung it at a university concert years ago. And if the opportunity arose, there was the matter of the school choir.

He was joined by the attractive dark haired soprano he'd noticed the previous week. He offered to buy her a drink but she said she was OK and was waiting for one of the tenors.

115

Five minutes later the aforementioned tenor turned up and Mr Carlston discovered she was called Susie and the tenor Nigel. He noticed Jenny and the pianist come through from the lounge ready go upstairs so he followed them to discuss singing the solo. There was also the question of under-age sopranos he wished to raise.

Chapter 25 : Mr Thicket's Invitation

Tim found Mr Thicket's house without difficulty. It was larger than he'd expected. He noticed with approval the well kept garden and wondered if Mr Thicket did it himself or was it his wife. He went up the drive to the front door and rang the bell. After a few moments the door was opened. It was funny seeing his old teacher in a cardigan and slippers.

'Come in, Come on in', said Mr Thicket. He admitted Tim to a large and very tidy hallway. 'Come through to the lounge. Would you like some tea?'

The house was clinically tidy. There were fresh flowers in a vase which Tim liked on the table and a couple of excellent paintings on the wall but it was not at all how Tim had imagined it. It was certainly unlike the chaotic art room back at school. 'Please sit down', came Mr Thicket's voice from the kitchen. 'Do you like your tea strong? Did you find the place OK?'

Tim was looking at some photos on a book case when Mr

Thicket arrived with tea and a plate of cakes.

'Your wife, sir?' he asked politely.

'My late wife, Catherine. And the young lady is our daughter, Charlotte, Charley to her friends.'.

'She's very good looking,' said Tim and meant it.

'Yes, gets that from my wife. Come and sit down, she's away in Bristol at the moment. At the university.'

'Is she studying art?'

'No, English literature. My wife wrote a number of successful novels, you know. But Charlie isn't particularly artistic. Now, tell me about this exhibition.'

'Well it's on October 10th and 11th at the Hornwood Gallery, but you'd only need to come on the Saturday. Just for the opening. 11 in the morning. I'm not actually sure where the gallery is is.'

'Oh, I know it. In Fitzwilliam Street. That's a very good place. So what do you want me to do?'

'Well, Mr Pointer said I needed to find someone who could introduce me as an artist and as you were the one to start me off, I can't think of anyone better. Perhaps it would be better not to mention the monumental masonry too much. A five or six minute speech if you can think of anything to say about me.'

'Oh I'm sure I can.'

'So you'll do it. Oh thank you, sir. I'll ask Mr Pointer to send you an invite. And would your daughter like to come?'

'I doubt it. Not in term time, although I think that's the

beginning of half term. And you can't keep calling me 'sir'. It's Frank.'

'Right, Frank. This is a lovely house. Do you live here by yourself?.'

'I do, ever since Cathy died. Charlie came up last weekend and spruced it up a bit – brought in the flowers and so on. I doubt she'll be back now until half term, or even Christmas. And now I only work part time at the school I enjoy doing the garden myself'

'It's a credit to you,sir'

'Frank'

'Frank'. It was going to take time for Tim to become comfortable using his old teacher's first name.

Chapter 26 : Tamsin's Photocopies

By the time Thursday came round again Tamsin had managed to photocopy all the music. When Jenny asked about the cost Tamsin smiled and said that Littlestone High School where she worked liked to support the arts even if at times it didn't know it was doing so. Jenny questioned the morality of this but Tamsin said it would be much harder to explain now it was done and she couldn't take the copies back as they would be no use to anybody there.

Although they had arrived early, Tim had already set out the chairs and was back downstairs chatting to Sam and Carl behind the bar. And a keyboard had appeared which Tamsin tried and declared more than adequate. They went back downstairs and asked Sam about the keyboard.

'Ah, surprise from Mr Braithwaite. He reckons it was being unused in one of his other pubs and it would save you lugging yours in each week.'

'Well you just tell him how grateful I am, we are,' was Tamsin's response.

There were already about thirty of the choir in the lounge including a middle aged couple each holding a glass of wine who singled Jenny out.

'Can we have a word, please?' asked Valerie.

'Of course,' said Jenny, just remind me who you are.'

'Oh we're the two Vals, she smiled, ' but it's not about us. I used to be a teacher locally and I recognised one of my ex-pupils last week'.

'And is that a problem?'

'No, you don't understand, I think she's only 14 or 15. So what with this being a pub'

'Oh I see. But if we're talking about Sophie, I think that's her father who comes with her.'

'No, no. Not Sophie. Colette. Colette Milner'

'But we may have a solution.' It was Mr Val this time. ' If someone is that determined to sing we are happy to act as responsible adults for her.'

'Now we haven't spoken to her about it yet,' It was Mrs Val again, 'and we would need to speak to her parents but we thought we'd check with you first.'

'Well that's very kind of you both and I very much appreciate you taking this trouble. She certainly looks older.'

'That would be the make up', said Mrs Val, as Mr Val took a mouthful of wine, 'and a pair of socks, I suspect.'

Mr Val blushed and choked slightly on his wine.

And as if on on cue, Colette came into the lounge. Valerie and Jenny went across and after a brief conversation, Jenny left them to it. So she could go and explain to Tim that he didn't need to set out the chairs by himself every week but realised she had as little chance of dissuading him from doing that as she had of stopping him calling her 'miss.'

The lounge was filling up rapidly as she moved into the bar where she was immediately button-holed by Richard Carlston.

'Ah, Mr Carlston, can we nip upside and have look at the three kings carol?' she asked.

120

He followed her up the stairs , 'Before we start, Jenny, I think you ought to know that one of my pupils has joined the choir pretending to be over 16.'

'Yes, I know; Colette, but Mr and Mrs Valentino have kindly agreed to act as responsible adults so that little problem is solved. Did you say you had sung this piece before?

'Yes, when I was at university.'

'Well let's just try the opening.'. She switched on Tamsin's keyboard and played a chord of G major. 'In your own time.'

'Three kings from Persian lands afar..' Whilst not brilliant it was confident and evident that he had sung it before. She played the choir part for a few bars then stopped. 'That's going to be fine. We'll try it later with the choir.'

'Don't you have to audition other people?' he asked.

'No. you're the only volunteer.' There was a sound of footsteps on the stairs. ' Here come the others so we'd better make a start.'

Chapter 27 : Colette's Journal

September 21st.

Hermione Smyth was sick in maths this morning. I asked her if she was up the spout but she said she couldn't be. And I believe her because what lad's going to do it with her. And she's got a copy of that Kes book now from the library.

Been to that choir again. Shaggzz was there and he sang one of the solos beautiful. The rest of us choir are like his backing group.

Mrs Winston who used to teach us English but stopped being a teacher when her husband died is in the choir. Now she's called Mrs Valentino.

I used to think she was a stuck up old bitch but she's really nice when you get to know her. She'd grassed me up for being under 16 but then offered to be my 'responsible adult'. Don't know exactly what that is; it's like when social services or the police come for you but it's different because it means I can keep on coming to the choir.

There's a short woman that I think Shaggzz fancies but she's more interested in a posh guy called Nigel. That suits me. Mind you, that Nigel is a bit of a pain. He keeps interrupting with silly jokes that nobody understands. Like when Molly,the tall girl that looks like a model, was showing us her new tattoo. He said he'd thought of having a tattoo for his birthday but decided not to because he couldn't stand bag-pipes and his garden wasn't big enough.

Actually Molly's a bit of a laugh. She wanted to do some actions to the two front teeth song. Every time you sang 'two' you had to stick two fingers up and then point to your top teeth.

I thought it was hilarious but the rest didn't so I don't think we're going to do that.

Jenny says they are doing a cheap student rate for the choir so I only have to pay a small amount to join. It's the first grown-up group I've ever joined and the singing's a lot more fun than I expected so I reckon I'm going to join proper. It's funny. When the lads at school interrupt lessons with their funny comments it makes me laugh but when Nigel does it at choir it irritates me. I want to tell him to shut up and be more grown up. Mrs Winston says he is used to talking in public because he's a barrister. I thought he was a lawyer. I can't imagine him serving drinks.

Mrs Winston is going to come round and see my mum about being my responsible adult. I'd better make sure the house is clean and tidy first and not too many of mum's cider bottles are around. I don't think I can get rid of the smell of fags. I got some pictures from Miss Holden about what smoking does to your lungs but mum wasn't interested. She reckons if you're going to get cancer you'll get cancer, whatever you do. That doesn't seem right to me.

School's having a Hallowe'en do next month. Tom Clancy asked me if I wanted to go to it with him. I said I'd think about it.

Chapter 28 : Susie's Statements

The fourth rehearsal had gone well. Tim had finished stacking chairs and had gone down to the bar and Tamsin and Jenny were left re-checking the money.

'Well that all tallies. Now do you believe we have a choir?'

It was difficult for Jenny to disagree. 97 full paying customers, most already paid up till Christmas plus three students. And even after only three rehearsals they were beginning to sound confident.

'I'll get this into the bank first thing tomorrow.' Jenny said.

'Are you OK about taking it home by yourself?' There was concern in Tamsin's voice. 'I didn't expect so may to pay in cash.'

'Oh I'll be OK . Even the choir won't know which of us is taking it and nobody else knows I've got it. But I won't stay socialising tonight as I've got a couple of private pupils early tomorrow. See you next Thursday.' She left Tamsin packing her keyboard and at the bottom of the stairs shouted 'Cheerio, everybody!'.

A few people shouted back or waved, and she left the pub. Although it was late September it was still warm and dry but already dark..

She had only gone a few steps when she became aware of a small middle aged man as he came towards her.

'Excuse me, miss, I'm looking for Jasmine Street.' He was close enough now for her to smell his aftershave. She turned to point behind her and before she had time to think she was grabbed and she could feel cold metal by her throat.

'Now just let go of the bag and you won't get hurt'. She forced herself to relax her grip on the bag and she felt the knife being taken away. As he released her she turned back to see her assailant as he moved away. The next few seconds passed in a haze. By now he was moving off with his back to her and she couldn't see his face. Then she became aware of a huge shape which flew past her and hitt her assailant like a tank, flattened him to the ground and sat on him. In the same instant she saw the knife fly into the air and clang into the gutter. And finally a welcome voice she recognised said, 'You alright, Miss?'

'Tim, is that you?'. It could hardly have been anyone else.

'Yes Miss, don't you worry, I've got him. Can you get somebody from the pub to help and call the police.' But the police, in the form of Susie Blake were already there. She and Nigel had just come out of the pub and she instantly had her warrant card out.

'I'm the police,' she said, ' what's going on?'

'This guy's just tried to rob me. He had a knife- I think it's in the gutter over there. And he got my bag but Tim turned up out of nowhere and stopped him.'

Tim looked a bit overawed by this sudden attention, particularly as other people from the pub were beginning to gather around and form a crowd. And someone produced a camera . within the next few hours one particular photo made the local morning paperl. It was Tim, literally sitting on the mugger, with the caption 'A Truly Monumental Mason',

'Are you really a policeman?' he asked.

Nigel leaned closer to Susie and quietly suggested she'd better arrest the mugger before the weight of Tim killed him. 'And it might be an idea to caution him.' he added.

Susie had never done this before, 'I'm arresting you on suspicion of an offence under the1980 theft act. You do not have to say anything. But, it may harm your defence if you do not mention when questioned something which you later rely on in court. Anything you do say may be given in evidence.'

Nigel spoke again. 'Now unless you carry handcuffs in you handbag, I should phone the station and tell them you need back-up. Tell them you have a prisoner.'

Somebody shouted, 'There's a knife over here', and Susie called, 'Don't touch it. Has anyone got a clean plastic bag?'

The next half an hour were very busy. Eventually a police car arrived and two policemen took charge of the mugger and took statements from Jenny and Tim. Technically the handbag was also evidence but Susie allowed Jenny to remove the contents The knife was transferred to an evidence bag and finally the car departed with its prisoner.

Those that were left returned to the pub. Tim was the hero of the hour, despite saying he only did what anybody would have done.

Jenny, who had been OK up to that point suddenly began to shake. Someone suggested giving her a brandy but Sam produced a cup of tea which while it was more of a builder's brew than Jenny was used to certainly helped to calm her down.

Susie thanked Nigel for his help and said, 'I don't think I need to go into the station straight away even though I'm the arresting officer. A couple of hours in custody won't do him any harm. So what's your unofficial opinion of our mugger?'

'I'm thinking exactly what you're thinking. He's so like Timmy Madison I thought it was him. And the same MO. Perhaps that jury got it right after all.'

'Amazing there were two of them who look alike and use the same trick. Do you think they could be related?'.

Tamsin had her arm around Jenny's shoulder and was arguing that she should accompany Jenny home. Several others were supporting this view when Tim banged the table and said, 'I will take miss home.' in a voice which, although quiet, brooked no argument.

Mr Carlston was relieved he had not carried out an earlier plan to ingratiate himself with the short dark haired woman by offering to share his recreational chemicals. And now he realised that she was the one he had noticed patrolling the school parking. Funny how different she seemed out of uniform.

Chapter 29 : Jenny's arrangements

It was the first time Tamsin had been to Jenny's flat. They had decided to have a working meal before the rehearsal. Tim had been persuaded that Jenny didn't need a bodyguard to and from every rehearsal and Jenny had told Tamsin that the police had said that the mugger, who it turned out was called Steven James would be tried in the Crown Court because he had a weapon and because he'd done it before. So it wouldn't be till after Christmas.

On the choir front things were looking very positive. Mr Crowther was one of only two who had not signed up last week but he had said he often had meetings on a Thursday so that wasn't surprising.

Tamsin had noticed Mrs Valentino preventing Colette buying a cider in the pub so the responsible adult arrangement was obviously working.

Sam said that Mr Braithwaite was more than happy for the pub to carry on hosting the choir until Christmas.

The Vicar of Doom was happy for the choir to perform in the nave rather than the lady chapel, Tamsin translated these as main church and little room at the side for Jenny's benefit. They would have to raise some extra lighting from somewhere.

Richard Carlston was OK as the soloist.

There wouldn't be enough material rehearsed for a full concert so they would have to fill the rest of the programme somehow. Tamsin suggested Jenny do some solos but Jenny wasn't happy about that. She wondered if some of the choir would like to do solos but after the response or rather lack of it over the

Cornelius that didn't seem likely to produce much. They could share the programme with another choir but there didn't seem to be one. Tamsin's school didn't have one. The Vicar of Doom had already described the departure of the choir from St Peter's and Jenny knew that Brunswick didn't have one because Mr Carlston was trying to persuade her to start one there. She was planning to meet the headmaster after half term, but even if they started straight away they wouldn't be ready for Christmas.

They decided to mention these things to the choir. Because it was coming up to the half term break everyone would have an extra week to come up with solutions.

Over a pasta meal Jenny asked what Tamsin was doing during the short holiday and when Tamsin said, 'Not much', she explained that she had booked a cottage in the lake district for a long weekend and wondered if Tamsin was interested in sharing it. Tamsin said she was but would it be OK for her boyfriend to come as well. This was the first time Tamsin had mentioned a boyfriend and Jenny realised how little she actually knew the girl sitting opposite her. She said it would be fine if they were OK sharing a room. Apparently Stuart managed a small theatre, which meant he did everything from booking the performers to sweeping the floor. And, importantly, he had a large estate car so could take them all.

The discussion then went back to the Christmas Concert. What were they going to do about refreshments? Were they going to serve them in the church? Would the Vicar of Doom allow alcohol? And did Jenny know if the church had loos?

How were they going to sell tickets?

It was round about then that they realised that what they really needed was an official treasurer or administrator. The choir needed a separate bank account and some means of paying in the money without Jenny or Tamsin taking the risk of carrying it around.

And were they going to produce flyers to advertise the concert?

As they walked from Jenny's flat, Tamsin asked about her family. Jenny explained that she didn't expect any of them at the concert. Her mum and dad had never liked her moving away from Wakefield and realistically it was a long way for them to come. Tamsin began to think that the split was far from amicable and this was confirmed when Jenny let slip she had not seen her family for the last eighteen months. They wanted her to get a proper job and thought the big city was a den of iniquity. She didn't mention the sudden death of her younger sister and her irrational jealousy that a dead sibling was receiving more attention than the surviving one. It had been a difficult time for all of them.

She did share that her parents had first met in their church choir and that her dad managed a local co-op store and later mum had a part time job on the checkouts. She didn't mention that the church had not really helped with Christine's death and the aftermath.

They spent the rest of the journey discussing individual choir members. Both agreed that Mr Carlston was a bit full of himself but was adequate for the Three Kings Carol. Jenny asked if Tamsin thought anything was going on between the little soprano Susie and the tall tenor Nigel and Tamsin said she thought there was. They both laughed about the Valentinos who they now knew were not married and lived at separate addresses. Tamsin commented that the girl who described herself as an actor seemed to spend most her time working as a hair stylist.:

Once they reached the pub they were instantly engaged with members of the choir and quickly shepherded everyone upstairs and into the warm up routine. Tamsin was always surprised and impressed by the range and variety of activities that Jenny could produce to exercise the choir's vocal spectrum before rehearsing the actual pieces.

Tonight the first piece was a nice arrangement of 'I saw mummy kissing Santa Claus'. It had a jazzy piano accompaniment which was fun to play. She noticed that it seemed to upset the young girl, Sophie she thought was her name but the librarian lady passed her a tissue and said something which seemed to sort it out. The gay couple shared a joke about it. Richard, who she had now learned was the music teacher at Brunswick looked slightly unwell.

The piano was near the altos and she recognized one of them as Barbara who worked in the cafe near the cemetery just up the road from Littlestone High She liked the sound of Barbara's voice. It had a natural warmth and she sang in tune, which, it had to be admitted, was not true of all the singers.. And Tiny Tim was smiling, but then he usually did. It was odd, when you considered that much of his job involved commemorating dead people. It didn't seem to affect him although he didn't appear hard or uncaring.

The first half of the rehearsal had gone well when Jenny took the usual break.

'Ladies and gentlemen, much as we are enjoying ourselves there are a few business matters to sort out. Tamsin and I have been chatting and we wondered if anyone here was prepared to be the choir's administrator and treasurer. That could be two

131

separate people of course. As we've got half term coming up with no practice next week, it gives you time to think about it. I've set up a group email to make it easy to get in touch but if anyone can set up a web page or facebook or such, please let me and Tamsin know by email. Also we haven't got a name for the choir yet, so you can email us that but please, no choiry-mc-choirfaces or silly names like that.. And finally, does anyone fancy having a go at being our announcer on the night – telling the audience about the pieces we're doing and so on. Right, restart in five minutes.'

During those five minutes a number of problems were resolved. Miss Ferguson offered to be the joint administrator and Phoebe offered to act as the announcer. Carl explained he was an IT manager and if someone told him what they wanted he could probably set up a web-page. Miss Ferguson asked Carl if he could help her set up a computer accounts system. When asked if she had a lap-top or PC she realised she had neither but resolved to treat herself.

Chapter 29 : Stefan's stamps.

Stefan had just finished his Saturday morning shift and had left the depot on his way home when he noticed a crowd in the market place. As he got closer he could hear drumming and then other instruments. They were playing for a strangely garbed group with jackets with long ribbons hanging down which spiralled out as they danced. Added to the noise was the sound made by sticks which the dancers clashed together. By now he could see that the dancers had elaborately painted faces matching their red a green costumes.

Curiosity led him to move closer.

A woman dressed in the same uniform as the dancers came up to him with a bucket marked 'Children in Need' with a bandaged teddy bear on it and persuaded him to give up his 'loose change'. 'What is happening?' he enquired.

'We're Molly Button morris dancing for charity. It's our last dance out of the year.'

'It looks fun,' said Stefan, without realising he was thus unwittingly sealing his fate.

'We're about to do a joining in one,' said the woman, and before he knew what had happened he found himself thrust into a sleeveless jacket with lengths of material stitched to it, a large hat unceremoniously placed on his head and a stick pushed into his hand. Five minutes later, with minimal instruction and gales of laughter he was, along with the rest of Molly Button completing a simple dance together with an older lady and two children who had been equally plucked from obscurity. At any moment he thought he was about to have his fingers broken but the dancer facing him was more cautious when hitting than appeared. Similarly there was a lot of stamping and he worried that his toes might be crushed. However, when the music stopped, his hands and feet remained uninjured. So that was OK.

As he took off the hat and jacket he could hear someone telling the audience that that was it for this season and thanking the four volunteers from the audience.

One of the Molly Button men collected his hat, jacket and stick and told him that the tradition after morris dancing was to go into a local pub and one way and another, twenty minutes later he found himself clutching a beer sitting in the pub at the centre of a recruiting drive which Lord Kitchener would have envied in World War one.

One of the women came across and asked his name and he responded 'Stefan'.

She burst into laughter, ' Stefan? I thought it was. I remember you. It's Emily; Emily from the English classes'. There followed lots of 'What have you been up to?' 'Are you still a postman?' and he was introduced to the rest of the dancers. He remembered Emily telling him about morris dancing. So this was it.

Sucked in by the atmosphere, and possibly the effects of the second pint someone had forced into his not-unwilling hands. Stefan finally asked, 'Where and when do you meet? If I wanted to join.'.

'Well,' said Emily, 'Wednesday is our practice night, but the church hall, a prefab hut, where we practised last winter is being pulled down so they can build something more permanent. At the moment we're looking for a new place.

'How big a space do you need?'

When they told him the upstairs room at The Crown where the choir met sprang to mind. He said, 'I have an idea.'

Names and phone numbers were exchanged and eventually Stefan was able to continue his journey home. Only he didn't go home. He went to see Sam at the Crown.

So it happened that two and a half weeks later Molly Button held their first Wednesday practice upstairs at The Crown. And they welcomed their first ever Estonian member. Sam reckoned that although there were only twenty of them they made more noise than the Thursday evening choir and drank more beer. Stefan thought it was OK.

Chapter 30: Jenny's maps

Stuart, Tamsin and Jenny set off for the lakes early on Monday morning. It was raining. Although the traffic was heavy they had passed the M62 in good time and by half past two had found the cottage. It was still raining.

On the journey Stuart and Jenny had got to know each other a little and Stuart floated the idea of the next choir concert being performed in his theatre. Jenny thought this was a distinct possibility but wanted to get the first one out of the way before spending too much time planning a second. There was also the issue of the size of the choir and whether the theatre would be big enough.

The cottage turned out to be larger than they had expected. Stuart and Tamsin took the slightly roomier bedroom leaving Jenny the one with the view out over Windermere. The view would have been magnificent. Only she couldn't see it for the rain.

But within half an hour Stuart had found the log store and got a fire blazing in the living room hearth and Jenny and Tamsin had produced broth and bread. At about half past four, the rain abruptly stopped, the sun came out and the three were able to take advantage of the stunning views. They decided to go for a walk along the edge of the lake for a while. Shortly after leaving the cottage they passed a pub which they earmarked to drop into on the return journey. Although it was October, it was not too cold but they decided not to stay out late and they were glad to be back in the pub just before seven. The pub was not as crowded as it would have been at the height of the tourist season, and the landlord was able to provide them with a vegetarian meal, albeit a bit basic. After a couple of drinks they ambled back to the cottage. Stuart built up the fire and he and Tamsin cosied up on the sofa. Jenny had brought 'The Grapes of Wrath' to read and settled in an arm chair. By nine-thirty all three had dozed off and it was only when Stuart needed the loo and disturbed them that all three came to and officially called it a day.

On the Saturday the weather was fine so they walked from the cottage away from the lake and up into the hills. On the way back they stopped at the pub again to discover it was Karaoke Nite. All three of them entered and Jenny won ten pounds which they used to help buy their evening meal and drinks. While they were drinking a man they took to be a farm worker aged about 30 came across.

'Enjoyed your singing, ...Jenny isn't it'

Jenny recognised a slight welsh accent and a possible attempt at a pick up line.

'Thank you, do you sing?'

'Not at the moment. I used to. When I was at college. It's about time I got back into it.'

Jenny's stereotypical view of agricultural colleges conjured up a group of rustics with pints of cider singing in a barn.

'Which college were you at?' she asked to be polite.

'Well I started at Magdalen, in Oxford, but I finished my training in Edinburgh. I used to sing in St Giles.'

'Are you a vet?' asked Tamsin who felt she vaguely recognised the man but couldn't place him.

'No just a humble GP. The name's Trev by the way. '

'What, you're the local doctor here?' Tamsin was fascinated.

'No, I'm here visiting my gran. She thinks she runs the local haberdashery shop.'

'How do you mean 'thinks she runs'?' It was Jenny's turn.

'Well she turns up every morning and unlocks the shop – it is, after all, her shop - then she sits there all day while my Aunty Margaret does all the work. But all gran's cronies pop in for a chat and a browse, so gran thinks she's busy dealing with custotmers. They never buy anything. Not that there's ever a lot of work for Aunty M serving the few tourists who call in. And when gran finally shuffles off I imagine Aunty M will inherit the shop'.

'It's very good of you to visit her.' Stuart joined in.

'Not really. Mixing business with pleasure. I own two or three cottages round here which I let out. I'm staying in one for this weekend.'

'So where is home when you're not here?' It was Stuart again.

Trev decided it was his turn 'Dahn Sarf', he effected a pantomime cockney accent. 'And you three. Do you sing regularly?'

'Not me,' said Stuart, 'my partner here, Tammy, is the accompanist for a choir that Jenny here runs. I'm Stu, by the way.'

'Pleased to meet you, Stu.' The two men shook hands. 'And is this choir local?'

Before Stuart could reply Jenny who had been in a reverie blurted out, 'You're Doctor Trevor Owen.'

The other three were taken aback.

'Yes, I am.', replied Trev 'Are you claiming five pounds?'

'You're one of the doctors at the Brunswick Practice.'

'I am. Are you one of my patients?'

'No,' Jenny replied.

The scales fell from Tamsin's eyes. 'No, but I am. Well not one of yours but of Doctor Cummings.' She had sat in the waiting room looking at the photos of the staff long enough for his face to be stored in her subconscious.

'One of Amanda's? What an amazing coincidence. She's my fiancee. But,' turning to Jenny, 'if you're not one of my patients how did you know my name?'

'It all makes sense now. I'm Jenny Lint, I saw your advert in the newsagents for the cottage. We're actually your tenants at Rose Cottage until Friday.'

'Small world,' said Trev. 'So that means your choir is local to me, or at least where I work. Now I'm a bass baritone so what are your basses like?'

'Well there's Bill Crowther who between these four walls has a range of about 5 notes and couldn't hold a tune in a bucket without help,' said Jenny with unusual candour. Then there's Tim. He's very quiet but works hard and seems competent enough. Oh and there's Bob the Blaster. He's West Indian and doesn't read music but rote learns everything and is then worth any two other bases. Then there's Shaggzz.'

'Who on earth is Shaggzz?'

'Oh that was his name when he was in a group.'

'Not the Toxic Wasters?'

'I think so. Why? Do you know them?'

'Very much my generation,' said Trev. 'I remember him having his biking accident and breaking both wrists and elbows. He left the group after that. I didn't know if that was because he couldn't play any more or if while he was recuperating the band found somebody they liked better. So what's he doing now, apart from singing in your choir, of course?'

'He teaches music at Brunswick High. His real name is Richard Carlston.'

'Good Lord. Richard Carlston is really Shaggzz. This just gets better and better. Amanda and I know him, in a professional sort of way. Look I must go round to my gran's now. She'll stay up fretting till I do, but are you guys going to be in here tomorrow – can I buy you dinner? About half past six and you can tell me how to join your choir. Cheerio.' And as they answered cheerio, they could hear him wishing everybody in the pub goodnight. He was obviously well-known and well liked there.

'Well,' said Jenny, we spend a fortune on flyers around the neighbourhood and end up recruiting in the Lake District'.

On the Sunday they followed the same pattern but walking much further. Jenny could feel the stress of her life-style rolling off and hoped Tamsin and Stuart were having an equally good time. They stopped to take pictures of the birds, the landscape and the ferry plying its trade across the lake. They were back at the pub at 6.30 to find Dr Trev, as they had begun to refer to him, already settled in the bar chatting to a couple of the locals. He had obviously changed clothing from the previous day but still managed to look like a farm labourer. Part of it was his weather-beaten features. In Tamsin's experience most doctors

140

spent too much time indoors and didn't have the opportunity to weather very much. He had a round, ruddy face and wore a leather waistcoat and corduroy trousers with a wide leather belt. And boots. If they didn't have steel toe caps, they looked as if they should.

He ordered drinks for them all and then said, 'Right, what are we eating then? I could eat a horse.' Jenny pointed out that that was out of the question as both she and Tamsin were vegetarian. He guffawed at that and asked if Stuart was of a similar persuasion. Stuart said, 'Not yet, but Tamsin's working on it'.

Eventually they ordered and while they were waiting Dr Trev entertained them with tales of his life as a medical student. He was a natural entertainer and both Jenny and Tamsin thought he would be an asset to any choir but particularly theirs. When Jenny broached the subject he said it was virtually a done deal. He had already spoken to Amanda who was apparently a very competent alto and she was keen to come along too. Because they could both read music, they didn't think it would be too much of a problem catching up on the missed rehearsals. Dr Trev did warn them that occasionally they might be a bit late if surgery over-ran.

During the meal, Dr Trev asked if the cottage had been OK. Stuart said it had been really comfortable and all three agreed it was very conveniently placed for the lake and the village. Stuart said its only disadvantage was how far he had to drive to get there. And to get home. Eventually they left, wishing each other goodnight. 'See you a week on Thursday at practice,' was Dr Trev's farewell.

On the following day they spent the morning relaxing around the cottage. After a late brunch Stuart and Tamsin set off leaving Jenny behind. Jenny said she had some songs to learn and needed to catch up on her correspondence on her lap top. They agreed to meet at the pub at six thirty again.

As they walked Stuart asked Tamsin if Jenny was seeing anyone and Tamsin said not that she knew of. She told Stuart about Jenny coming from Wakefield but said she really didn't know much about her. 'Mm,' said Stuart, 'a woman of mystery'. Whilst no more was said about it Tamsin did start to think that she ought to get to know Jenny better as a person. Whenever they were together they usually only talked about the choir or singing. And even then Jenny had never mentioned where she had trained or how she had learned to inspire people as she did.

Meanwhile, Jenny spent time learning half a dozen songs she wanted to try out in a couple of weeks time when she had three pub bookings. She'd already asked Tamsin to accompany but Tamsin was away on the Friday so could only do Saturday and Sunday. Jenny emailed two or three other pianists she'd worked with previously. She also started to put together a programme for the choir next term and began to source the music. She knew if the Christmas concert was a success she would have to come up with a bigger event for Easter. Before she realised it the clock said twenty five past six so she put her coat on, locked the cottage and hurried to the pub.

By now it was quite dark and she was surprised Tamsin and Stuart weren't there already. Several of the locals said hello as she made her way to the bar. She ordered her drink and as she served her, the barmaid said, 'Your two friends not with you?'

'No, they went for a walk and we agreed to meet here at half past six. So they're only five minutes late.' She took her drink to a table and, sitting down, she tried to phone Tamsin's number

142

but got diverted straight to voicemail.

'If they're up on the hill they probably won't have a signal,' said the barmaid.

Ten minutes passed and there was still no sign of them. By five to seven, Jenny was becoming quite worried. It was some relief when Dr Trev appeared through the door. 'Hello again,' he said, 'Where's Stu and Tammy?'

'I don't know, and to be honest I'm a bit worried. They went for a walk and we agreed to meet here half an hour ago.'

'OK. Do you know where they were heading for?'

'No, they didn't say.'

'What kind of equipment did they take?'

'Not much. To be honest I didn't pay much attention. They just took a sort of picnic.'

'Well if we're going to organise a search party we need to do it before the cold of the night settles in.'

'A search party?' Jenny was suddenly afraid.

'I've got the Landrover outside with basic emergency kit in it.'

However, at that moment, the half formed idea of a dramatic rescue was destroyed when the missing couple walked in through the door.

'Sorry we're late,' said Stuart. 'Oh, hiya, Trev. We've just come from your gran's house. She invited us in for tea and she was telling us all about the history of the place and her family...What?' He stopped abruptly.

'We were getting ready to send a search party for you,' said Jenny partly relieved and partly furious over the unnecessary worry., 'Why didn't you phone?'

'We tried, about twenty five to seven but you were obviously still arranging the concert and things because it went straight to voicemail. You'll see you've got a missed call if you look.' said Tamsin.

'Can I get you two a drink,' said Dr Trev to ease the situation.

'Definitely our round,' said Stu and took their orders.

After the first drink, Dr Trev said he had to talk business to another landowner in the other bar and left them. Stu then arranged food for them all but after that they decided to go back to the cottage early because they had the drive home the next day. As they left they shouted cheerio to everyone. Passing the door to the other bar they could see Dr Trev deep in conversation with a stunningly beautiful woman. 'I wonder if Dr Amanda knows about her,' thought Jenny.

On the Tuesday they had just finished tidying the cottage and loading the car when the rain returned. It lasted for most of the journey home but Stuart played music in the car and the two girls sang for much of the journey.

Chapter 31: Miss Ferguson's P45

While Jenny, Tamsin and Stuart were recharging their batteries in the Lake district other members of the choir had mixed fortunes. Mr Spooner at the library had been offered early retirement which he'd taken and Dot Parker's first action as the new Chief Library Assistant was to make Miss Ferguson redundant. With immediate effect.

Carol eventually did the translation for Justine Buckley . Having emailed the finished document he decided to go and buy something for his tea. Almost accidentally six weeks ago he had given up smoking. He had smoked his last one and forgotten to buy more. That was the moment when he decided to try and give up. He must be careful not to be tempted into the newsagents although he suspected that Mr Nowicki already sold cheap cigarettes under the counter anyway.

When he reached the store, Mr Nowicki handed him a letter which had been left for him by 'someone in his choir.' He hoped it was the little soprano who ran the children's dance classes and always looked as though she needed cheering up but it was from the tall guy, Nigel. They had spoken very little at choir as Nigel was busy chatting to the lady policewoman so he was very surprised when he opened the envelope to find a note asking him to phone. He came out of the polish grocers and although he was proud of having resisted buying any cigarettes he had bought a bar of chocolate and a packet of licorice alsorts. He must start watching his weight. And he didn't want to trade the risk of lung cancer for the risk of diabetes.

As soon as he got home he telephoned Nigel to see what he wanted. It turned out that Nigel had a Polish client and the solicitor had never dealt with a translator before. He wondered if Carl was interested in becoming accredited as a court translator. The pay wasn't wonderful and the work irregular but it would perhaps put him in touch with other people who needed a translator. Carl said he was interested but what he really wanted to do was use his computer qualifications. Nigel said he hadn't realised that he was in that line of business. His chambers were currently looking for a part time IT manager. They finished the phone call by arranging a meeting at Nigel's chambers with the Head of Chambers and the Clerk for the following afternoon. Nigel said he would phone with a time after he'd been into chambers and arranged it. Carl wondered if he could get through the next twenty-four hours without a cigarette. Nigel wondered if Susie would like a weekend away somewhere. He considered Paris.

Tim's exhibition had exceeded his wildest expectations. The local paper had covered it and he'd even given an interview over the phone to the local radio station. And he had sold many of his pieces.

He had arrived at work on the Tuesday still full of high spirits to find an urgent message on his answerphone. When he responded it was to a solicitor, a Mr Patel, who had bad news. Mr Jolley had had another stroke from which he had not recovered. Mr Patel was looking after Mr Jolley's affairs and wondered if Mr Dalby could come to the office to see him as soon as possible. Tim agreed to close the business early and go that afternoon.

After he had put the phone down he started opening the mail. Amongst the usual invoices and payments was a letter from a

Mr Thomas, the headmaster at his old school. It was an invitation for him to join the governors at the unveiling of the replacement foundation stone. The headmaster apologised that they were not able to remove the original so were putting Tim's next to it. The only problem for Tim was it would mean closing the office for another half day in a couple of weeks' time. He didn't know how to employ people and he didn't have many friends to ask but perhaps someone at the choir might know. Or he could ask Mr Patel. But solicitors were expensive. He would see how the meeting went. He knew as a partner he would still have half a business but it might depend on who he was now a partner with. He knew Mr Jolley had neither wife nor children but he vaguely remembered Mr Jolley once mentioning a brother.

Susie had done another stint at the school and passed another piece of useful information to Criminal Intelligence. Sergeant Oldman had been quite complimentary. And later that day Nigel had phoned and offered to take her out for a meal. That was something to look forward to.

As there was no choir practice on the Thursday evening Mr Rossini had invited Mrs Winston to a night at the opera. It was the full works. Somehow he had managed to obtain two good seats at Covent Garden for a performance of La Boheme. He explained that the last time he had seen this opera was as a young man with his mother at La Scala in his home city. When they came out it was slightly chilly and Mr Rossini insisted on singing 'your tiny hand is frozen' all the way back to the tube. To emphasis the point he took Mrs Winston's hand which was neither tiny nor frozen. She didn't object.

Pauline spent Tuesday afternoon at Nikki Philips house. Nikki had recovered fully from her fall and the baby within her was progressing well. Pauline had visited her on the ward on the day after her collapse and a strong friendship had developed over the next few weeks. This was helped by Nikki's assertion that she was never coming back to the day ward which Pauline saw as an indication that the job was hers.

Chapter 31 : Sophie's Card

The first rehearsal after half term started, not with the usual warm ups but with a rousing chorus of 'Happy Birthday to You'. Somehow, Miss Ferguson had discovered it was Sophie's 13th birthday and had secretly primed the choir. They had brought cakes for the interval and everyone had signed an enormous card with music notes and a cute picture of Sophie aged about three in the middle of it which had been supplied by her father.

Jenny had arrived at the Crown to find Sam in a bit of a panic. As it was mid-October he had decided to put the heating on, only to discover the boiler wouldn't fire up. He had lit log fires downstairs but had only managed to find an inadequate fan heater for upstairs. He apologised, particularly as the fan bit was rather noisy. Jenny had told him not to worry, it would be good practice for the performance in the cold church. She would make the warm up slightly more energetic than normal.

After Happy Birthday it was the energetic warm up Jenny had

promised and then back to the concert programme. The sopranos had clearly done a lot of work as individuals on the descant to O Come All Ye Faithful, and by the break time Jenny felt that the Cowboy Carol had made more than satisfactory progress. In fact the whole choir was beginning to sound like one big voice and not a lot of individuals. She suspected one of the altos whose name she couldn't remember but who always stood next to the Indian lady spent a lot of time miming but overall they worked very hard. The choir could now manage all the pieces so it was time to give them some light and shade. She explained that p meant quietly and f meant loudly. Nigel instantly offered, 'Easy to remember, you p softly but you f loudly.' Jenny ignored the interruption.

Dr Trev and Amanda had turned up true to their word and not only was Dr Trev a natural leader for the bass line but Dr Amanda was a perfect fit to lead the altos. Jenny suggested that as they were only coming for half the term they should only pay half the fee but Dr Trev said that as they still needed all the music they should pay a full subscription each and instantly handed over a cheque for them both. This was handed to June Ferguson to put into the newly opened bank account. She had arranged for herself, Tamsin and John Turner to be the signatories. She flipped open her shiny new laptop and registered the payment in her spreadsheet. Bless Carl for his help.

There was another new member, a tenor, Philip who was Stuart's brother. It turned out that after the holiday, Stuart had spoken enthusiastically about the choir and Philip decided to give it a try. He did only pay half fees.

At the interval, before the choir was released to the cake Jenny started as usual, "Ladies and gentlemen, much as we are enjoying ourselves there are a few business matters to sort out. First, while we are a large choir, our repertoire is not so large. So to fill up the evening performance I've been racking my brains trying to think of another local choir or band who might be suitable and willing to share the platform with us. Also, we ought to invite some local big-wigs. Does anyone know how to get in touch with the Lord Mayor?'

Many of the choir broke into hysterical laughter and Jenny looked round bemused.

'What? Did I say something funny?'

Bill Crowther pushed forward from the bass ranks and said, ' Jenny, there is no Lord Mayor in this borough, just a mayor and,' stroking his bald head, 'no wig, big or otherwise. Next week I shall be inaugurated as that Mayor and I have every intention of attending the concert – but in my usual capacity as a bass'.

As Jenny spluttered her apologies, Bill continued, 'And, as you have raised the matter, on the day after our concert, it is my privilege to arrange the switching on of the Christmas Lights in the market place. I am delighted to invite this choir to come and sing carols at the informal ceremony.' This was greeted by warm applause above which Jenny could be heard saying 'Back in 5 minutes everybody'

Much happened during those five minutes. First Kim cornered Jenny and suggested that her group, Kim's Kidz could do the other section of the programme. Jenny thought that might be a solution to her problem. Kim knew it would be the solution to one of hers. When she mentioned the need for some kind of extra lighting in the church, mayor-elect Bill said to leave the lights to him. 'Trust me, they will be there.' Unlike most politicians, Jenny felt she could trust this one.

June Ferguson was asking Sophie when she had last been on a shopping trip and suggesting one for the following Saturday as a birthday treat. She suggested they finish it with an early evening showing at the cinema. She would ask Mr Turner to arrange for the other paper girl to do both rounds for a bit of extra cash.

Nigel was checking if Susie had ever been on Eurostar.

Tiny Tim wondered if Mr Carlston had ever met Mr Thicket's daughter, but Mr Carlston said he didn't even know that Frank had one.

Carl spent the time, and part of the second half taking photos for the web-site he was working on. He took several of Kim on the grounds she was likely to be bringing her dancers.

Jenny began to realise that this choir had begun to pull together as a team even if with vicars without collars and mayors without chains you couldn't tell who's who any more.

Chapter 32 : Mr Jolley's will

Tim was in the headmaster's office at his old school. Mr Thicket was there and so was Mr Carlston from the choir. They were all drinking sherry after the unveiling of Tim's foundation stone. This was all very uncomfortable for Tim. Last time he had been here it was to say farewell as he set off on his apprenticeship. In those days the headmaster had been Mr Walker but today the post was held by Mr Thomas.

Now Tim was becoming a well known local artist and the outright owner of the only monumental mason business for miles. The meeting with Mr Patel had gone really well. It turned out that Mr Jolley had left him not only the business but also his house, its contents, his huge collection of classical music CDs and, which came as a surprise, his car. Tim had never realised that Mr Jolley drove anything other than the works old van, much less that he owned a 1933 Bentley, immaculately preserved in his garage. Tim was waiting for an expert in such vehicles to come down from Manchester before he even dared to try starting the engine.

After the meeting and acting on Mr Patel's advice, he had asked at last week's rehearsal if anyone knew of an office worker looking for a job and lo and behold Miss Ferguson had 'just become available from the library service' and had started on Monday on a three month trial. She had instantly persuaded him to buy a computer and set about organising the paperwork and accounts. She was happy to have the music CD going on in the background and the only problem was he missed the phone calls from customers because by Wednesday morning she had got most of that organised as well.

Today he had been able to leave the business open so he could attend this event with a clear conscience and Mr Crowther, the new mayor, who was also there, had wondered if he might be interested in standing for the local council. Tim had never had any interest in politics but he had promised to think it over.

The event had gone well, he thought. It had been decided not to remove the original foundation stone but to put Tim's slightly to the right of it. Tim believed this was an excellent idea, rather like a translation.

Mr Thicket interrupted his thoughts and invited him outside for a minute. 'Best leave the sherry glass here', he had said.

Outside there was small, squat lad of about 16. 'This is James', said Mr Thicket.

'Hello, James,' said Tim, not sure where this was leading.

''During one of our earlier conversations, you mentioned the possibility of an apprenticeship.' said Mr Thicket.

'That's right, I did,' Tim remembered.

'Well James might be interested. If we can arrange a convenient time perhaps James and our Ms Stephenson – she's our careers teacher now - could come to your office and discuss it. That's if you are still looking for an apprentice'.

With everything else going on Tim had completely forgotten the idea but this lad didn't look the usual dis-spirited teenager.

'No promises,' said Tim, 'but if James and Miss Stephenson want to come tomorrow afternoon, that would be fine. I don't suppose James has already done anything like this?'

James shook his head.

'Well wear scruffy clothes and we'll perhaps try something

153

then. See you tomorrow, James.'

Tim and Mr Thicket went back inside.

'Thank you for remembering, sir.' said Tim

"Frank'

'Frank,' said Tim. He realised that during the entire time he'd been outside. James had not spoken a word.

As he retrieved his sherry glass, Miss Bunce the school secretary hurried in. To Tim as a pupil she had seemed to be part of the fabric of the building but he now realised she was probably only 7 or 8 years his senior. Her attributes which had led the adolescent boys to nickname her Miss Buns were still very much in evidence.

She apologised to the headmaster for interrupting but felt he would want to know that the police had just arrested a young man outside the school gates for dealing drugs. Some of the older pupils said it was Matthew Holland, an ex pupil and brother of Christine Holland in year 8. The headmaster made his apologies and left with Miss Bunce.

Mr Crowther said, to no-one in particular, 'About time the police earned their keep.'

Chapter 33 : Tamsin's flyer

On the last Saturday in October Jenny had sung at a sixtieth birthday party and had invited Tamsin to accompany her. On this occasion, apart from payment, they had also been offered a meal afterwards as part of the deal. Thus it was they found themselves in a luxury hotel out in the countryside. Over the meal they discussed the plans for the choir's Christmas concert and particularly the advertising. They also discussed giving the proceeds from the concert to a charity and Jenny suggested the Samaritans. Tamsin thought this was a good idea as it lacked any kind of political overtones but Jenny said it was because of something some one had said. Tamsin didn't follow it up instead asking if Jenny was in any relationship at the moment. Jenny said that she was too busy and offered nothing more so Tamsin decided not probe.

Jenny wondered if they should plan some kind of Christmas social but Tamsin thought the choir could do that for themselves. But they did decide to ask Sam to lay on some nibbles for them after the concert so they could all go back across the road once they were finished.

Finally they discussed what the choir should wear. Tamsin suggested Christmas jumpers as they would be both colourful and warm. Jenny thought that this was a wonderful idea but excused herself because she said she always got very hot conducting. She put forward the suggestion that they record the concert in some way but they decided they hadn't the time to organise it properly. Jenny said she would put together the programme before the next rehearsal.

By the time Stuart arrived to take them back to Tamsin's so that

Jenny could get a taxi back to her flat they felt that they had the concert evening mapped out. Tamsin had agreed to design a poster and over the next couple of days she and Jenny emailed designs back and forward until it was complete, apart from the name of the choir, which had still not been decided. There was just the word 'The' followed by a space.

To save time, Tammy took it on CD to the printer she had previously used and said she would email the choir name as soon as they decided on one. Tom, the guy she knew at the printers, said that would be OK and put a post-it on it saying 'choral flyers, 250 copies'. That way she could email the name and whoever was going to set up the print run would know which disc contained the poster.

Chapter 34 : Sophie's recipe

Tears rolled down Mr Turner's cheeks. He had never been in this situation before. Normally he closed the newsagents at about 3 o'clock on a Sunday. Then officially he spent the afternoon on the accounts for the week. Unofficially he sat on the couch watching TV until Sophie finished her homework and provided an evening meal. But now he and Sophie stood facing each other across the kitchen table as she supervised him slicing onions.

'Enough?' he asked.

'Should be. Now put a little oil in the frying pan. And while that's warming, let's get the rice started.'

156

'What if she doesn't like onions?'

'Dad, I've checked.' Sophie was slightly exasperated with her father, 'I asked her. She's OK with everything except mushrooms and some sea foods. And she doesn't like apricots. That's why I thought you could do Mediterranean Chicken. It's easy'

'I still don't know why we're feeding her.'

'Because she's coming to sort the choir accounts and, if there's time, to have a look at the shop's.'

Indeed, it was a moot point who had been most surprised, June Ferguson on being suddenly invited to a late Sunday lunch, or John Turner on finding himself inviting her. Sophie was totally unsurprised.

Apart from organising her father to produce the meal, Sophie had also given the living room and loo a thorough going over and bought some flowers from the local garage to brighten the place up. Her dad had asked if that was what they did for a visit by Miss Ferguson, what would they do if the queen was coming? Gold plate the bath taps? But ultimately he knew Sophie would get her way. Fortunately, at this moment he didn't know what Sophie's master plan was. Actually, neither did Sophie, not in detail. This was one of the occasions when she missed her grandparents. She often thought of grand-dad with his quaint sayings from a bygone age. In her present undertaking 'slowly slowly catchee monkey' sprang to mind. She didn't really know how adults went about these things. She didn't want to remove the photographs and other visible evidence of her mother but she didn't want anything to cause Miss Ferguson to ask questions that would set her dad off maudling. That was another of grand-dad's words. In the end she left the photos where they were and placed a vase of flowers in front of them.

She wondered if putting a CD of romantic music on would be too much but when she looked at her dad's collection of old rock albums she decided it wasn't an option.

She got the best china out of the cupboard where it had been unused since her mum left. She took it into the kitchen and started washing it.

'Why are you washing that?' her dad asked, 'It hasn't been used.'

'Oh Dad, it's all been in that cupboard for months. It will be dusty. Poor Miss Ferguson is already going to be at risk of poisoning with your cooking without there being germs already on the plates. I don't suppose we have any wine do we?'

'No, we don't.'

And then the doorbell rang and there was Miss Ferguson who had not only put on her best suit and gloves, but also carried a bottle of wine.

'I don't know if this is appropriate but if not, your dad can drink it during next week.'

'Please, come in,' said Sophie. 'That is a lovely idea and will go well with the meal my father is cooking.' She had no idea whether that was true but it sounded like a sophisticated thing to say.

As she led Miss Ferguson into the living room she called, 'Dad, Miss Ferguson's here.'

'Sophie, I think it's June from now on, for both of you, don't you.' The older woman smiled a knowing smile which the younger returned. Sophie liked this woman. She hoped her dad would. As John Turner came in Sophie went to keep an eye on the food and wash three wine glasses which had not been used for many months. Then she thought better of it and took just two glasses and a bottle opener through to the adults.

'Dad, if you do the wine shall I serve the food you've cooked.'

'Yes, that would be good. Thank you, Sophs'. He felt out of his depth but June Ferguson chatted to him about the choir accounts as he opened and poured the wine.

Sophie served the food and they all settled round the table to eat. June complimented John on his cooking whilst Sophie thought how nice it was to have three people around the table again.

After the meal she said she would do the washing up whilst the adults got on with business and when she had done that she went upstairs to finish her homework. Mission accomplished.

June Ferguson produced her laptop from her shoulder bag and she set about educating John Turner in the mysteries of computer accounting. She started by stressing the importance of security and logging off whenever you left the computer. She didn't feel comfortable enough yet with John to share the Craig Madison story.

It was John who later suggested that the system she had devised might also work for his shop and the two of them started on that. Eventually, John said it was time for coffee. While they were drinking John suggested that she might like to come round one evening to continue with the shop accounts and they settled on the following Friday. June said she would bring a take-away for the three of them so they could tell her what they fancied on Thursday at choir.

By the time June called, 'Goodnight,' up the stairs and left, Sophie had dozed off.

Chapter 35 : Tim's policy documents

' A Ms Stephenson and James O'Brien to see you,' smiled June Ferguson ushering in the young lad that Tim recognised from the previous day. Tim noticed that James, far from coming in scruffy working clothes as he had suggested, was wearing smart school uniform. He wondered if that was the school's decision?

June offered them tea but was politely declined so after arranging chairs for them, she sat herself at her computer and carried on creating order out of chaos with some of the accounts.

Ms Stephenson, who was white and had once been described as 'ethnically dressed,' wasted no time in getting down to business. 'Thank you for seeing us both at such short notice,' she said.

'You're welcome, Miss Stephenson, I suppose we need to sort out a date for James to start.'

'Well there are a number of questions to sort out first. And it's Ms by the way.'

'Sorry?'

'Ms. Ms Stephenson.'

'Oh, sorry, well what are your questions Ms Stephenson?'

June noticed the emphasis on this last 'Ms' by her employer and recognised it as a sign of irritation.

'Well, firstly, Mr Dalby, there is the issue of health and safety.'

'Oh that's easy,' said the unsuspecting Tim, ' Don't drop the stones on your foot because they're bloody heavy and don't cut yourself on the chisels because they're bloody sharp'.

Ms Stephenson bridled. 'I'm afraid it's not as simple as that. I need a proper health and safety policy document for my files. With a risk assessment.'

'I'm not sure we have..' started Tim

'Mr Dalby can let you have that by Monday.' Miss Ferguson had taken up the cudgels. 'As a reputable Monumental Masons we are, of course, members of all the relevant trade bodies and party to their practices agreement including their guidelines on health and safety.'

Ms Stephenson was almost as dumbfounded as Tim but recovered more quickly.

'And do you have a designated health and safety officer?'

Tim opened his mouth, ready to put his foot in it, but June got there first.

'I shall be taking over that role from Monday. As Jolley's has only been an employer for a matter of days we had to take advice on this, again from our trade organisations because, as I'm sure you appreciate Ms Stephenson,' like her boss emphasising the Ms a touch too much, ' it is better to get these things right first time.'

Ms Stephenson recognised a worthy opponent when she met one.

'And what about discipline and complaints?'

'We are establishing the recommended ACAS three-step procedures, which I'm sure you're familiar with.' June at last was beginning to appreciate all the hours she'd spent in endless meetings on such matters in the library service. She was just inwardly praying that Ms Stephenson wouldn't ask what the three steps were because she couldn't quite remember. Tim, meanwhile, realising he was outclassed, sat back to enjoy the fight and considered how lucky he was to have found Miss Ferguson so quickly and easily. He was glad she was in his corner.

Looking at the three other white people in the room Ms Stephenson moved on, ' And how do you implement the equal rights act?'

Tim would have liked to say that most of his memorials were for dead people, all of whom had an equal right to be dead, but knew it would be a mistake.

'Considering the only two applicants this business has ever had for apprenticeships came from your school, Ms Stephenson, and both were white and male I think we should, perhaps, be asking you the same question,' June was beginning to enjoy this.

Tim was a bit lost on this. Was there another lad. He only knew about James. Two candidates?

Ms Stephenson side-stepped. 'For instance, I couldn't help noticing that all the background music constantly playing here is Western European for example. Do you have any plans to introduce any world music? I mean this current noise is hardly appropriate for today's youth, coming as it does from years of oppression from European empire builders.'

Tim had finally worked out that June was including him as one of the two apprentices when this assault on the great Jolley's classical music tradition was made. But as he drew breath to defend his beloved CDs and as Miss Ferguson searched her vocabulary for a reply, a voice said,' It's the Chorus of the Hebrew Slaves from Nabucco.' And after a stunned silence, 'By Verdi'. It was the first time Tim had heard James speak. 'He was an Italian writing an opera about Jewish slaves in Babylon. That's pretty good world music I reckon.'.

June recovered first.

'We also offer a pension plan once James qualifies, sick pay, and statutory paternity and maternity benefits. It is always comforting to know that if one became pregnant, one would have both the emotional and financial support of one's employers, don't you think.' June delivered this in a tone which suggested it was even less likely Ms Stephenson would end up pregnant than she would, and she was 45. Game, set and match, she thought. And so, apparently did Ms Stephenson.

'Well that all seems perfectly - adequate. How soon can we get the documentation sorted and James started?' she asked.

'I think a week on Wednesday morning would be fine, don't you, Mr Dalby'

'Well, er, yes, if you think so Miss Ferguson.' and recovering his composure, 'and thank you both for your time,' he said, rising to his feet to indicate the interview was over. Miss Ferguson left her computer and held the door as the two visitors left.

163

The moment the door was shut Tim demanded 'Now what's all this about trade organisations and policies?'

'Don't worry, Mr Dalby', there must be some and I will look them up on the internet and get all the certificates we need. But I think a nice cup of tea, first, don't you?' She busied herself with the kettle and two mugs.

'What happened to 'Tim'?'

'I think it's Mr Dalby in the office and Tim at the choir. And I think we ought to at least get some china cups and saucers for when we have visitors.'

'Yes, OK,' said Tim, 'And after all that I'm sure I can leave you to organise a bit of crockery. You have carte blanche.' This was a phrase he'd only recently learned from Mr Patel, the solicitor. 'Now you'll excuse me while I go and carry on with the Coulson epitaph, Ju - Miss Ferguson'

'Of course, Mr Dalby. Do you happen to know whether the O'Henrys have paid for the work you did in August?'

'If it's not in the income book then no they haven't. The book may not be state of the art but it is meticulously accurate. You know, that lad didn't come dressed to work as I suggested. I wonder how much of that was because of the dreadful Ms Stephenson?'

This was the first time June Ferguson had ever heard Tim suggest that anyone was less than perfect. 'It's probably a school policy, Mr Dalby. I shall send the O'Henrys a gentle reminder about their bill.'

As they walked back to the school Ms Stephenson was considering making a compilation of world music CD to send to Mr Dalby via James on Monday morning

164

James was thinking that he knew a far better recording of the Nabucco than the one on the CD at Jolley's and wondered if Mr Dalby knew about it.

At the same precise moment Tim Dalby was thinking what a pity June Ferguson had stayed single as she would have made someone a good wife. In less than a week she had reorganised the office so they could both work in it and set up a computer accounting system.

June Ferguson was thinking she was happy that she had the choir accounts organised, and was establishing a basic system in the Jolley office . Now she could give some thought to her developing relationship with John Turner and his daughter Sophie. She could see several ways of revitalizing the ailing newsagent's shop. Tonight she was providing them with a takeaway meal and on Sunday she thought she might arrange to pop round and make a casserole for the three of them while she discussed an idea she'd had for using Sophie to deliver choir publicity along with the papers.

It was hard to realise that less than a fortnight ago she was being made redundant from the library. Well they say a week is a long time in politics.

Chapter 36 : Tamsin's leaflets

For once, Jenny arrived at the rehearsal before Tamsin so decided to have a soft drink downstairs before starting the practice. Many of the choir were already there and Carl came to serve her at once.

'Hi Carl', she said,' are you good?'

'Never better,' he said. 'This is a lucky pub,'

'How do you mean?'

'Well first it got the choir. And then it got me this job. And now I'm doing some work translating at the law courts and I've been interviewed for the post of IT manager at a barrister's chambers. And on Tuesday we started our Polish dominoes club here,'

'I don't think I've ever played Polish dominoes.'

'Well, it's the same as...Oh I see. A joke. Anyway I expected about 10 and there were twenty-seven people. I ended up behind the bar again. Hello Tamsin.'

'Hi Carl. Jenny, I need a word.'

Something was obviously troubling her friend who was carrying a large and evidently heavy box.'

'What have you got there?'

'I got a message from Tom at the printers this afternoon that my flyers were ready.'

'They can't be. We haven't chosen a name for the choir yet.'

'That was my immediate thought, But, well, have a look. I'm so sorry.'

Tamsin pulled a flyer from the box and handed it to Jenny.

A Christmas Concert by The Choral Flyers, read Jenny.

'That stupid lad down there thought the post-it on the box was the name of the choir. And they haven't time to reprint them for another two or three weeks and...'

'Hang on. That's not a bad idea for a name. More zippy than the Crown Community Chorus, and it gives the impression of sort of soaring up in the sky and freedom and rising above things. Don't panic. I reckon we could stick with this. We'll ask the choir at half time.

'Excuse us'. It was Dr Trev and Dr Amanda.

'It'll have to be quick, because it's nearly practice time'. And she noticed that already the crowd in the bar was drifting up the stairs.

'We just wondered – well next April, would the choir be interested in singing at a wedding.'

'I can ask them. Whose?'

'Why ours.' said Amanda.

'Oh – congratulations, both of you.'

'To each other', said Trev.

'Yes I realised that. Will it be local?'

'Yes we hope so. We're thinking of Brunswick Hall or the old Roxy Cinema. Now we were wondering what you would charge?'

'I don't think we would charge. I mean, we're not charging for the switching on of the Christmas lights.'

'Oh we insist on paying you for your time, at least', said Amanda.

'We'll discuss it when we've more time. But well done both of you. Now let's go sing.' Jenny closed the conversation firmly and put the memory of the woman in the lake district to the back of her mind. She turned and headed for the stairs, leaving the others to follow.

Once again, the rehearsal started with 'Happy Birthday' and the promise of cake at the interval. This time in honour of Mr Rossini.

'And now, to get us into the Christmas Spirit and start the warm up, everybody stand up and follow me.' It turned out that surprisingly few of the choir already knew the actions to the Twelve Days of Christmas and whilst great fun was had improvising increasingly complex harmonies for 5 gold rings, a different kind of hilarity ensued each time they arrived at 6 geese a-laying and did the faintly vulgar squatting with elbows out as wings. Tamsin happily improvised an accompaniment.

Finally they settled to working on the pieces for the concert until the inevitable

'Ladies and gentlemen, much as we are enjoying ourselves there are a few business matters to sort out.'

'It's always good to start with joyful news so I am delighted to announce the forthcoming marriage of Dr Trevor Owen and Dr Amanda Cummings of this parish next spring and,' a tide of applause and cheering was starting to rise,' Our choir has been invited to sing at the ceremony.' There was louder applause and cheering at this.

And at last we have a name. How do you feel about 'The Choral Flyers'.

'Is that with an 'i' or a 'y' asked June Ferguson.'

'Show them a poster, Tamsin'. There was more applause for the poster.

Bill Crowther shouted 'I declare this choir open.'

Nigel added 'And God bless all who sail in her.'

'We'll distribute them at the end.' said June Ferguson, restoring order, 'And if I could have a quick word,' and without waiting for a response 'Tickets will be available from Mr Turner or me from Monday and Mr Turner's shop, the newsagents will act as our box office. Oh, and Sophie will deliver some of these flyers with her newsround.

Chapter 37 : Sara's compositions

The following evening, Sara was upstairs at a different pub, The Sultan of Egypt, preparing to sing. This was the Pyramid folk club's monthly meeting and she was the warm-up act in the first half. The stars of the evening, the Moonstones, were on after the interval. Nina introduced her and she started her set, five songs she had written herself.

They all had a political flavour to them. The first was about the rights of women and was receiving its first outing. Sara was looking forward to seeing how it would be received.

She had already recognised a smattering of members of the Thursday choir who had come to support her including the young man she now knew was listed among the tenors as Jason Kirby.

The first song had gone well. The second one she'd written to commemorate her great great aunt who had served in Belgium as a nurse in the first world war.

She followed this with a song about a still-birth. Although mercifully she had no personal experience of this she felt she had crafted a well structured lament.

Her fourth song, by contrast, was a comedy song about a woman called Sally who received a shoe catalogue and ordered a pair from it. The audience laughed at the trials and tribulations of Sally's attempts to get a matching pair that fitted.

She finished her set with a song about 'the strong women of history,' which had a chorus for the audience to join in. She was delighted when they did.

She left the stage to generous applause and went to join the other members of the choir by the bar.

As she approached Jason said, 'Well done, Sara. I think I owe you a drink so what are you having?'

'A half of bitter, er, Jason isn't it? And why do you owe me one?

'In the cemetery. You gave me your number, remember?'

'What's this?' said Michelle, one of the sopranos, 'A choir romance we know nothing about?'

'No', said both both Sara and Jason simultaneously and not quite convincingly.

'It was to do with the choir,' improvised Jason, 'You gave me a poster and I'm afraid I lost it.' He turned to the bar to order her drink.

'Oh, yes, I remember,' said Sara carelessly, although something inside of her was delighted that this might be a genuine reason why he hadn't called. She turned to the girls, 'Well thank you all for turning up to support me. I hope you didn't think it was a waste of time.'

'Have you written many songs,' Josie asked.

'About 30'.

'You could do an album', said Naomi.

'I didn't know you could play the guitar,' said Josie, and Michelle added, 'You ought to offer to Jenny at choir to do it in The Cowboy Carol.'

'Sounds good to me,' said Jason.

By now the Moonstones were on stage and tuning up and the

audience settled down for the rest of the performance.

Afterwards, it turned out they were all going the same way home so they left the pub together. They reached Jason's road first and he wished them all goodnight. 'Cheerio, called Sara, 'and thank you for the beer.' She regretted not finding an opportunity to give him her phone number but that would have probably been too pushy and the rest of the girls would have taken the mick.

So it was only when she reached her own front door and was finding her key in her bag that she discovered a beer mat with a phone number written on it. She went to bed smiling that night.'

Chapter 38 : Phoebe's schedule

Phoebe, despite describing herself as an actor, had not attended that many auditions so was delighted to receive a phone call from a company called Razmataz. They would like to see her the following afternoon with a view to joining a Theatre in Education team visiting primary schools.

Her first reaction was to check on the internet that they were a legitimate company. They seemed to enjoy a reasonably good reputation so at 3.30 she presented herself at what appeared to be an old school. There were two women about her own age already waiting. The first was tall and slender and was called in as Phoebe sat down.

The second looked to be in her mid forties and Phoebe wondered why someone of that generation was still trying for theatre in education but then realised that the first woman probably thought that about her. She knew people in that side of the business and understood it was exhausting. The acting played only a small part, really. More time was spent driving and setting up each show. And it was never above minimum wage.

About twenty minutes later the second woman was called and twenty minutes after that it was her turn.

She went into what had obviously once been a school hall but was now equipped as a rehearsal studio. There she met Stephen and his wife Jo who ran Razmataz. She was asked to perform her prepared speech and then to do an improvisation with Jo. Finally she was asked to imagine that she was doing a school performance. The play they were currently doing was based very loosely on the story of Dr Barnardo and the poor children of London.and she had to imagine her fellow actor, for some reason, missed his entry cue and left her stranded with a primary school audience. What would she do to keep the show going. She instantly went into The Twelve Days of Christmas with the actions as taught by Jenny. At seven swans aswimming Stephen gently interrupted her and asked her to return to the waiting room. This sounded good, she was to get an instant call back.

It was better than that. They asked how soon she could start rehearsals. And so Phoebe became a member of Razmataz. Two days of rehearsal and then three or four shows a week. The other girls at the salon would be happy to cover her clients.

After the rehearsals she was off on tour with three others, Claire, Edwina and Mike and from the first moment they got

173

on together. The first school they performed at was really pleasant and after the show the children asked for their autographs. The second was rowdier but the pace of the show soon engaged with the youngsters and as they repacked the props and costumes in the van it was agreed it was a success.
 Even better was the fact that before they drove off Mike who doubled as stage manager, Dr Barnardo, driver and general organiser handed his three colleagues their first wage packets. In an industry where invoicing performances and receiving payment was notoriously long winded, Phoebe realised that, while it wasn't the Royal Shakespeare, Razmataz might be just what she needed at this stage of her career.

Chapter 39 : Miss Ferguson's Tickets

By the next rehearsal the normal heating had finally been restored at the Crown. Everyone realised that the concert was looming close and there was beginning to be a feeling of tension. Michelle had emailed Jenny saying that she thought Sara ought to play guitar for the Cowboy Carol and after an email from Jenny, Sara had agreed to bring it to rehearsal.

This became the first item to practice after the warm up. Tamsin eventually decided just to play a simple um-cha accompaniment on the piano and let the guitar do the main work and the choir enjoyed the change of sound. Jenny suggested that Sara should sing one of the verses on her own and they rehearsed it like that. 'Please pencil that in your scores now', commanded Jenny, 'We don't want it turning into a duet, do we?' She smiled wickedly at one of the altos who at a previous rehearsal had, carried away by excitement, started the Three King's solo along with Shaggzz and then nearly died of embarrassment. Jenny had said that was OK but please not to do it at the concert.

Jenny had arranged that the Three Kings Carol would still be the opening number although in her heart of hearts she didn't think that Richard Carlston had really developed it much since the first run through. They rehearsed it again next and Jenny's opinion remained the same, Still, the choir had got the accompanying chorale well under their belts.

After Silent Night it was time for the break.

'Ladies and gentlemen, much as we are enjoying ourselves there are a few business matters to sort out. Mainly it is to urge you to get friends and family to buy tickets. June tells me they are going steadily but now we're committed to filling the whole church we need to sell a lot more. Secondly, I know we've suggested a choir uniform, but with so little time left can I suggest that we all wear a Christmas Jumper, the brighter the better. More importantly, it could be quite cold in the church so you can put layers on underneath. Colin has also said that there will be a Christmas tree. OK peeps, back in 5'.

The second half went like a dream. The choir was sounding secure and there was a rich tone developing. And Jenny noticed many of the choir had learnt their parts and only held the music in case they needed to glance down.

Chapter 40 : Mavis's receipt

Barbara had the cafe open and was putting up a poster in the window when Tina arrived. She stood outside and directed Barbara in exaggerated pantomime until the poster was straight. Then she came in.

'Morning, early bird.'

'Morning, Tina. Having a lie in, were we?'

'Somebody's bright this morning. Did we have a good sing last night?'

'It's really good. You ought to come along.'

'No. It's Joe's darts night. So is Ken being OK about baby sitting?'

'No problem. I think he's enjoying it. The kids certainly are.'

'That's good. And what about – is her name Emma?'

'Was. A thing of the past.'

'They've never split up?'

'It's a couple of months back. He told me when I first phoned him about the choir. Thought I'd told you.'

The conversation was interrupted by the arrival of customers, a couple in their thirties. Barbara served them while Tina hung up her coat.

'So what did he say when you asked him to have the children?'

'He was fine. He even picks them up and drops them off.' She decided not to tell Tina that when the first practice had finished late, he'd brought them to the practice and taken all three of them home. Or that two weeks ago he'd brought them to the practice and the four of them had eaten fish and chips in the car afterwards.

'So are you and Joe coming to our concert?'

'Oh I don't think it's Joe's scene. Anyway, he'll have to look after the kids.'

'The kids could come too. Mine are. It's not high-brow. Well, some bits are. The music teacher from Brunswick High is singing a lovely solo that we accompany. And there's one in latin. But then there's the cowboy one with a guitar and All I want for Christmas and a gospelly one.'

Barbara was interrupted by one of the customers who said, 'Is that the concert on the poster in the window?'

'Yes it is.' said Barbara.

'I might come to that. I only live round the corner from St Peter's. I saw the advert outside the church but I thought it might be … well a bit churchy if you know what I mean.'

'Oh it's not', enthused Barbara. 'And there's Kimz Kidz a local dance school.'

'Are they any good?' asked Tina.

'We haven't actually seen them yet; but they used to be in the panto at the town hall when there was one.'

'It's a pity there's not a panto this year,' said the customer. 'Freda and I have hardly missed one in the last ten years. Isn't that right, Freda?'

The customer identified as Freda was obviously used to being the silent partner. She smiled and nodded.

'Mavis, I said to myself, Mavis, now there's no pantomime what are you going to do with yourself. It looks like this is as near as we'll get, Freda. Anyway can't stay here all day chatting. Haven't you finished that coffee yet? How much do we owe you? '

Realising that the last question was aimed at her, Barbara quickly totted up the bill.

By the time the customer called Mavis had settled up, double checked the receipt and left several more customers had come in and all thought of Ken had left Tina's mind.

Chapter 41 : Kim's bills

'Hello, is that Mercedes?'

'Who's calling?'

'I'm calling about your internet advert for dancers'.

'Which one?'

'The gentlemen's club – in Hounslow'.

'Are you local?'

'To Hounslow, no'.

'Have you done this kind of work before?'

'No'

Kim's finances had reached breaking point. Kim's Kidz just about paid for itself but the supermarket wages did not cover her rent and her credit card was maxed out.

Mercedes continued, 'Right, well it's 50 quid every night to pay for your pitch. Anything over that is your take. No touching or 'extras', although away from the club your private life is your own. Nothing here though that would threaten our licence. You'd need to bring proof you're over 21.'

'So I pay you £50 just to work there.?'

'Yes. If you've tried other places you'll find we're one of the cheapest. And you get 10% of any drinks you sell. When do you want to start? I've got spaces Monday and Tuesday. 10 pm to 4 am'

'We'll say Monday then'.

'Don't forget your ID'

So it was that at 9-30 on Monday evening Kim presented herself at the Angel House Hounslow club for respectable gentlemen. By 10 past 10 she could not in her wildest nightmares imagine what a club for non-respectable gentlemen could be like. Maddie, one of the other girls had helped show her the ropes: told her never to use her real name; never accept a lift home, always carry mace in her handbag and who to speak to if she needed any tablets to keep her going.

At 4am after the longest night she could remember she had accumulated £120 from which she handed over £50 to Mercedes. She booked a taxi to take her home and at 4.30 the taxi driver, a middle aged sikh in a turban delivered her to her front door. At this point she discovered someone had emptied her purse of cash. She thought back and realised Maddie was the most likely suspect. She burst into tears.

'Was that your first night at that dreadful place', asked the driver.

'Yes – and last. And I have no money.'

'OK, so tonight I give you free ride. But you must never go there again. Promise?'

'Why are you doing this for me. What do you want?'

'I am a father. I have a daughter as your age. I want you to be safe as if you were her. And you will not be safe there – or anywhere like it. So go into your house. If they gave you tablets, flush them down the lavatory. Then sleep. And if ever I am asked to collect you again from such a place, I will make you walk. Do you understand?'

'I don't know how to thank you.'

'Do as I say. That is all. Goodnight, and good luck.' And he drove off.

Kim let herself in, took off her shoes, lay on her bed and cried herself to sleep.

Eventually she was awoken by the sound of the doorbell. She opened it to find a pleasant looking young man standing there with a smile.

'Hi, I'm Ben'.

'Ben?'.

'Yes. If you're Kim you gave me this address and told me to come round at 10 this morning'.

Vaguely the clouds were clearing from Kim's brain. Bill Crowther, the mayor had put Ben in touch with her to organise the lighting for Kimz Kidz. The light hurt her eyes so it probably was ten o'clock. She realised what a mes she must look.

'Tell you what,' Ben continued, 'I'll go and buy us both breakfast at the coffee shop down the road, come and join me when you're ready.'

Half an hour later, showered and with breakfast inside her, Kim's world looked a slightly better place. It turned out Ben ran a sound and lighting company which occasionally took students from the local college and gave them work experience. They were going to light the show as a favour to Bill Crowther who, as a governor of the college, had helped set up the scheme.

They were short of a vehicle to transfer the equipment. Kim thought of offering her car but apart from the fact that it was too small, she'd already decided that she needed to sell it to give her any chance of getting out of debt. So she suggested that Ben asked at the tomb-stone shop. She explained that the enormous man who worked there was a member of the choir and could probably help.

She also thought to ask if Ben could throw in a small PA system to play the CDs for Kim'z Kidz and he said he'd see what he could do. He had sensed something was wrong and asked her about her how she came to be running a dance school. She gave him a brief resume leaving out the previous night's disaster.

He listened patiently, then said, 'My girl friend may be able to help. She part runs a small video company and I know when I left this morning, she was still looking for a third dancer for a music video they are shooting tomorrow morning. Excuse me while I ring her.'

After a short call he passed the phone to her. Bea, the girl friend asked a few more questions then arranged the details of the shoot. It wasn't far from home, which was just as well as it was a five thirty in the morning start. It was in an industrial unit and would involve working on a routine with two other dancers. Once it was filmed, they would CGI the background then superimpose the singing star in front of it. So she would never get to meet the star.

Then there came the question of money. Bea, apologised that it wasn't a great deal for a 'buy out' then mentioned a figure equal to a month and a half's rent, half on the day and half when the client approved it. Bea also thoughtfully suggested that Kim bring a chaperone as it was early morning in a quiet area. Then she asked to be put back to Ben.

Ben finished the call and said, 'Right, I'm off. Perhaps see you in the morning, otherwise it'll be at the church on the day. Bye.'

Kim sat and thought for a minute. That's how a real gentleman behaved and wasn't Bea lucky to have found him.

As she came out of the coffee shop she ran into Carl from the choir who was looking very happy. He was going in the same direction as her. In the brief time it took to walk back to her front door he had told her that he had just heard that he was to be IT manager at a law firm so would be giving up work at the pub.

Kim went into her flat, re-did her make up and took herself down to the Crown. Sam looked worried and said they weren't open yet. She told him she had not come for a drink but for a job. Sam said he hadn't heard from Carl but when he did he would give her a ring. She left him her number.

Chapter 42 : Valerie's Christmas card

So here they all were at the last rehearsal. Amazingly they had only lost two singers since the first practice, a Jordan Clark who had only come to the three free rehearsals and an older lady called Moira who had just texted Jenny to say she had broken her wrist earlier that week and didn't think she would be fit for the performance.

Tim looked a bit down but explained that was because he had just started to make a memorial for Mr Jolley's grave as a final tribute to his former boss and benefactor.

Richard Carlston looked worried but Jenny put that down to stage fright.

They worked through the first half of the programme until the inevitable.

'Ladies and gentlemen, much as we are enjoying ourselves there are a few business matters to sort out. Now next Thursday's performance is at St Peter's Church. Do you all know where that is?' Since the steeple was visible from the pub window there was a burst of laughter.

'I'm delighted to confirm that Mr Braithwaite says we can come back here next term. So choir restarts on January 7th.'

This provoked applause and some cheering. There was consternation when one of the altos asked if the programmes had been printed yet. Tamsin saw the look of panic cross Jenny's face and said, 'June Ferguson and I have organised all that. ' She then held up a draft copy for all to see.

'OK,' said Jenny, back in 7.'

The next few minutes were taken up with several choir members passing Christmas cards to each other. Jenny found several on her music stand. There was laughter when it turned out Mr Turner had given June Ferguson an identical card to the one she'd given him.

Mr Carlston had an unsigned one he wrongly suspected had come from Colette. Sara thanked Jason for the card he'd given her and he thanked her for hers.

Mr Rossini and Mrs Winston were slightly embarrassed to receive two or three all addressed to Mr and Mrs Valentino.

Tim had given every single member of the choir a card but at least that meant no-one was left out.

Jenny thanked Tamsin and June for designing the programme which she secretly thought was much better than the one she had had in mind but had forgotten to put into practice.

And then it was back for the second half and by the time they went downstairs for a drink at the bar, Jenny thought they were ready. Well as ready as they were going to be.

Sam gave her and Tamsin a bottle of wine each. Jenny asked why.

'Because a few months ago, this was an empty pub with Colin often the only customer. Since you and the choir arrived we also have a dominoes club and a morris dance team and it looks like some time in the new year we're going to be a post office as well. I reckon that's worth a couple of bottles of wine.'

'I don't think we can claim responsibility for all of that,' was Jenny's response but to save further embarrassment turned and reminded everyone about the late afternoon practice before the concert and to wear Christmas jumpers.

She had her choir. Now she hoped there would be an audience.

Chapter 43 : Jenny's appointment

On the day of the concert, Jenny was running late by the time she arrived at the hairdressers. She was pleased to see someone had put one of her posters in the window. She sat in the waiting area half listening to the staff chatting as they worked and suddenly realised they were discussing one of her choir, Phoebe who was acting as compere that evening.

They were talking about covering Phoebe's shifts while she was doing her 'acting thing.' The one called Rosie said that she wouldn't have the courage to stand up on stage in front of all them people, and another said she didn't know how Phoebe could remember all them lines. Another, who according to her badge was called Pat, then mentioned that Phoebe was in a local choir and that's why she was off now, because they had a concert that evening. The second, Jamie, said she'd got a ticket from the newsagents because that nice Mr Carlston from the school was in it. Pat then asked if Jamie had noticed how much time the lady who used to work in the library now spent helping Mr Turner in the newsagents. Jamie said perhaps it was her job but Pat said that no it wasn't because she already had a job at the gravestone place. Jamie said she'd ask her Megan who was in the year group above Sophie Turner to see what the gossip was.

Then Jenny's name was called and she wasn't able to hear any more.

Meanwhile, Miss Ferguson and Mr Turner were finishing off the 'box-office' in the newsagents. Ticket sales were far better than expected. Pauline seemed to have brow-beaten most of the members of her church to come and there were all the parents of Kimz Kidz. Miss Ferguson herself had slipped into the library when no-one was watching and put up a poster. Most of the choir had bought two or three tickets each and Colin had said most of his congregation were coming, although that probably only added half a dozen. John Turner commented that the shop sales had increased noticeably as a result of the increased number of people coming in for tickets. June Ferguson suggested they look around for other shows they could sell tickets for. It was a pity the local pantomime wasn't happening this year. And perhaps they could suggest merchandising to the choir. T shirts and CDs? John noticed that increasingly June's ideas for the future included both of them but decided he didn't mind as her casseroles and more recently stir fries were making a pleasant change from Sophie's instant meals.

Tim was in his workshop supervising James on an apprentice piece. It was a nameplate for Hilltop, the name James's parents had ironically given their house at the bottom of Jasmine Street, itself an ironical name nowadays.

James was shaping up well, Tim thought then smiled as he watched the apprentice's hands shaping the stone. 'Shaping up well' was a good phrase. Handel's Messiah was sounding through the workshop and the two of them sang along from time to time, stopping to concentrate on tricky bits of the carving. Tim was carving 'Corbyn Place' in a complex cursive script as he sat opposite the lad. This was for the new student flats being built at the top end of Market Street. He thought about the company, Jolley and Son. One day he would have to change the name. Would it be Dalby and Partner one day? Who knew. His thoughts turned to Mr Thicket and from there to Mr Thicket's beautiful daughter, Charlie He hoped she would be at the concert tonight. He wondered if he had the courage to ask her out. He'd never risked asking a girl out before. He liked women, but was slightly in awe of them. Look how June Ferguson had organised his company – and the newsagent's if rumour was to be believed.

Then there was the formidable Ms Sullivan who had arrived with James. There was Jenny, his favourite Miss who everybody in the choir worshipped. And then he had come across Charlie. He hadn't even met her. But he knew if he did he would like her. And the chisel slipped and for the first time in his life he nicked his thumb.

Sara was re-stringing her guitar. She hoped it would settle before the afternoon performance.

Tamsin was leaving the doctor's surgery when she saw Jason. 'Are you on the way to choir?' she asked, a little superfluously.

'I am' he replied. 'I was hoping to meet up with Sara before hand for a quick drink in The Crown.'

'Sara, that's the soprano who plays guitar, isn't it?' said Tamsin who realised that she still didn't know half the choir's names including that of the young man she was with at that moment. 'It's terrible, I'm so busy playing for Jenny I know hardly anyone in the choir.'

Had Jason been in a PG Wodehouse novel he would have said, 'Sara is a goddess the ground on which she treads I worship. She has lips the colour of rosebuds and ears that are like mother of pearl.' He settled with,' She's the ginger one with the Birmingham accent.' They walked along discussing the choir programme with Jason suggesting future items. Tamsin hadn't the heart to tell him that following the appointment at the surgery this may be her one and only concert with the choir.

Valerie and Colette were sitting in the Vestry which had been designated 'Female changing room.' They had been the first to arrive. Valerie had been Christmas shopping and had decided she hadn't time to get home and then back to the church. Colette had come early to get out of her house. Both had removed their outer layer of clothing and Val was helping Colette with her make up. Colette suddenly asked, 'Why did you stop teaching us, miss?'

'Well you know I lost my husband, don't you?'

'Oh, we all knew that, it was in all the papers wasn't it?'

'Yes, it was. I don't know, I didn't feel I could face all the comments some of the children might make.'

'Is that it? Honestly miss, if I stopped going to school just because other kids made comments.'

'It's different for you.'

'Why, because I'm a kid? How does that make it different? We don't have a staff room we can go and hide in. So you gave up on us because of that.'

'Colette, I didn't give up on you. I gave up on me.'

'Well you're alright now, then aren't you. You've got your Mr Valentino fellow haven't you?'

'I suppose so, yes. And actually, his name is....'

'So when are you coming back?'

'What, to teaching?'

'To Brunnie '

'It's not quite as simple as that.'

'Why isn't it? Everybody knows Mr Carston is crap at teaching English. Sorry, miss, poor at teaching English. When I joined this choir he wanted rid of me. He told miss Jenny I was under age. But you, you and Mr Valentino, you bothered. You became my 'responsible adults.' You bothered to come and see my mum and dad. They won't even bother to come and see me sing tonight and, you know, I think this choir is the best thing I ever done.'

'Colette, I think this conversation you've just had with me may actually be the best thing you've ever done. Now look what you've done, I'm going to have to do both our mascaras again'.

Stefan was on his round delivering Christmas cards and parcels. He was pleased that most of Molly Button had bought tickets for the concert although he hoped they were joking when they threatened to come in kit. When she had discovered that he was going to be alone on Christmas Day, Emily had invited him to join her and her partner for Christmas dinner. So that was OK.

Carl had decided that while the courts were closed over Christmas he would do a thorough overhaul of the chamber's IT system. Nigel thought this was over and above the realms of duty but Carl was looking forward to using his expertise in peace and quiet. He realised it would be 3 months since he gave up smoking. Tonight was going to be a tough challenge on that score though. Nigel wasn't motivated enough to invite Carl to his family home for Christmas lunch. He planned, instead, to use the Christmas period to introduce Susie to his

189

family. He spent much of the morning looking for a nice piece of jewellery for her. It was too soon for a ring, he decided.

Susie was tidying her flat before leaving for the church. She felt her sergeant's exams had gone well and she hoped it wouldn't be too long before she got the results. Sergeant Oldman, for all his bluster, was one of the good guys and had pushed hard for her to be fast tracked. And DI Underhill had spoken on her behalf at CID if she chose to go down that route. It had been a funny few months. She had joined the choir believing she couldn't sing and now found herself leading the second sopranos. And she was beginning to be able to read music. She'd kept Sergeant Oldman to his word and got him a ticket although she suspected he wouldn't show up even though the choir had led to her making her first arrest. She had leave booked over Christmas and was looking forward to spending it at Nigel's family home in Norfolk.

Mr Val was talking to his late wife, Sylvia It was the first time he'd visited the cemetery without Val since their first meeting. He knew she would understand that his feelings for this new woman would never obliterate his feelings for her. Though they had no children, he could see that parents didn't love their first child any less when a second came along.

Kim was collecting together costumes and loading CDs into her car and hoping she could find somewhere close to park. She was also praying that Kimz Kidz would rise to the occasion with the extremely under-rehearsed dance nativity she had put together.

Pauline had put her feet up and had fallen asleep. She had done 5 twelve hour shifts last week and still managed to visit Nikki and the new baby and make the Thursday choir practice.

Because Phoebe's work was now mainly in schools she had taken the Saturday of the concert off from the hair salon and spent the morning practising the alto part along with the computer learning aids she had been sent a couple of months previously.

Trev and Amanda spent part of the morning visiting a possible venue for their wedding. They had found the old Roxy cinema which had been beautifully converted where the ceremony could be followed immediately with the reception. And there was a nice stage for the choir. They'd both then gone to afternoon surgery.

Barbara was wiping down the tables at the cafe. It was a busy morning with lots of Christmas shoppers and their parcels coming for tea and coffee. Ken had taken the kids to an artificial outdoor ski slope. She hoped none of them broke a leg. She smiled. Wasn't that what people said to actors before performances. Was the same true of singers. The manager was taking over at lunchtime so she could go home, change and get to the rehearsal.

Bill Crowther left the town hall at two. He knew he wasn't the world's greatest singer. If he was honest, he wasn't the choir's greatest singer. If he was brutally honest, he wasn't a singer at all. But he didn't half enjoy it. He walked down the high street and looked up at the Christmas lights and the huge tree. Tomorrow he would get Jenny to switch on those lights and the choir, with him in it, would sing. But before that there was tonight's concert. The Latin thing, Gaudete, and The Virgin Mary Had a Baby Boy were all very well but you couldn't beat the old favourites like Silent Night and O Come All Ye Fathful. And as he walked towards the church he started to sing.

Chapter 45 : The choir's programme.

The trip to the hairdressers had made her even later so Jenny hoped there weren't too many last minute issues to resolve before she could start the rehearsal. She'd had an urgent phone call from Dr Trev to say he and Amanda would have to miss the rehearsal because surgery was over-running but they would both definitely be there for the concert. There were at least 5 texts on her phone which she thought she would look at once she got to the church. It was cold and she was carrying her performance dress and shoes in one hand and the bag of her music in the other. She hoped someone had remembered the music stand which nowadays lived upstairs at the pub.

She crossed the road from the Crown and realised in the grey afternoon light that the church was brightly illuminated inside. The Jolley Monumental Mason van was parked outside which reminded her that Tim had agreed to transport the lights for them. Well at least that was going to plan. She wondered whether they needed to go back the same night or whether the Vicar of Doom was content to hold his service with them still there the following morning so they could be moved later. It would probably be OK if they were just using the little room for the service. She reached the door, remembering her first visit to this gloomy medieval building with the Vicar of Doom. Was that only three months ago? She opened the door and stepped inside.

There seemed to be activity everywhere. Sophie had set up a table just inside the door and was setting out a cash box, tickets and programmes. Miss Ferguson was setting out named envelopes with prepaid tickets in. Jenny remembered that John,

Sophie's dad, had said he wouldn't be able to shut up the newsagents until the Saturday sports papers were gone.

Behind them a small jolly lady Jenny didn't recognise was helping Carl unpack wine glasses on a table along with bottles of wine. She assumed it was Carl's mother. Two scaffold towers had sprung up either side of the nave and young men and women she didn't know were climbing all over them with cables and hoisting lights into position.

Tim, dear old Tim, was setting the chairs out for the choir. At the back of the church she could see Kim with her group of dancers gathered round her as she was giving them instructions. Mr and Mrs Valentino were putting up posters saying 'Toilets' 'Reserved' and 'Refreshments'.

Many of the choir were sitting in the main seats, pews she now knew they were called.

Everything looked organised and content. And then Tamsin came out of the lady chapel and dashed across.

'Did you get my text? Have you heard the news?'

'Well clearly not.'

'Mr Carlston's been arrested'.

'What?'

'For doing drugs. The guy they got outside the school had his phone number and details on his phone. He won't be here tonight.'

Jenny let out a word which would have shocked her parents and the vicar and probably many of the choir even if it had just been in the pub, never mind the church. She saw Tiny Tim raise his highbrows. Her voice had obviously carried. He started to come across.

'Is there time to ask Dr Trev?' suggested Tamsin.

'Dr Trev can't make the rehearsal and it's too high for Bob the blaster, even if he could learn it in time.. So that's the Peter Cornelius up the spout. And it was such a good opener. Even with an average solo voice.'

'I can do it, Miss'.

'That's very kind of you, Tim, but I think this is a disaster beyond even your powers to save us.'

'No, miss, I really can. It's one Mr Jolley had on a Christmas CD. I loved singing it.'

'Yes, I know Tim, but it's one thing to karaoke it on your own in your workshop but in a space like this and with an audience.'

Tamsin had gone to the piano and played a G major chord. And the world changed.

Jenny was not religious. She did not believe in miracles but there, in the church, at that moment something amazing and magical happened.

Tim opened his mouth and this huge and beautiful voice filled the building with a marvellous sound. Everyone stopped what they were doing and unbidden, with no conductor, on cue the choir came in with the chorale.

At the conclusion of the piece there was an awestruck silence. And then there was applause.

It was five minutes before order was restored and normal business resumed.

Jenny was almost in tears, 'Tim. Tim, why did you never let us know you could sing like that?'

'Well, miss, you kept stressing about blending in. Look at me. I'm not built to blend in. I've never blended in with anything. But then I joined your choir and you taught me my voice could. Blend in, I mean. And besides, you already had Mr Carlston. '

'Tim, I could kiss you.'

'Please, miss, don't. It would embarrass me. So am I singing it tonight?'

Jenny was beginning to well -up with emotion. 'Tim, of course you are. '

By now there was a queue of people waiting for Jenny's direction so she had to return to business mode

'OK, Tim, you're safe', she laughed. 'Right who's first?'

'Hi, I'm Ben and I'm doing the lights for tonight. I've already got a lights plot for the dancers but I wondered if you wanted anything special.'

Jenny had given it little thought and said that as long as the singers could see her and read their music and provided the audience could see the choir it would be OK. Ben reckoned he could do better than that.

Next it was the lady she had identified as Carl's mum who asked whether they needed any more mince pies. Jenny was amazed that the lady spoke with an Irish accent.

'I'm so sorry, I don't know your name.'

'It's Frances,' the lady smiled back. ' Colin should have introduced us. He never remembers.

'Colin?'

'Yes, I'm his wife'

The vicar of doom had a wife! It had never entered her head that Colin might be married – and certainly not to this round, happy woman.

'Whatever you think. June Ferguson is our treasurer – next to the girl doing the programmes. If you need some money.'

Time was getting on. 'Choir can we have you in position please. Let's start with a warm up.' She was aware of Kim's group at the back of the hall. Carl was down there helping hang costumes on a wheeled dress rail. She called, 'Do the dance children want to join in with this?'

Gradually order appeared out of the chaos. The children joined in the physical warm up and stayed for some of the singing warm up. They particularly liked the fun 12 days of Christmas with the actions. Some of the choir were coming straight after work and arrived in dribs and drabs, leaving coats and bags in the pews and slipping into place on the platform. Lighting came on and went off and on again.

By 6.30 Jenny decided it was as good as it was going to get and finished the rehearsal. She asked the choir to put their bags and coats in the lady chapel eat their sandwiches or whatever and be back by twenty past seven, in their jumpers, occupying the five rows which had been reserved for them.

The Vicar of Doom wanted a word. 'I wondered if at the end I might say a few words of thanks and perhaps explain about the work of the Samaritans as that is the charity you've selected to support.'

'That would be fine', she said, 'I've met Frances, by the way.'

'Oh indeed yes. The parish and I rely on her totally.'

196

There was a popping noise and all the lights went out. The children all squealed. 'Just a minute,' said a voice in the darkness, and a few seconds later the lights came back on. 'Just a trip going' said the voice which turned out to be Ben.

'Genesis 1:3', said Colin.

'Indeed', said Jenny, with a straight face.

She immediately took herself off to the ladies to change but looked up Genesis on her smart phone first. Oh, of course, 'Let there be Light.' She put her performance costume on. She'd chosen a trouser suit in white with small red and green sequinned decorations to give it a Christmas festive touch and a small silver brooch which her grandmother had given her years ago. Once she was changed and had finished her make up she went in search of Tamsin.

Tamsin was already dressed for the performance, having gone for a simple pale green dress with a gold brooch in the shape of a treble clef. She had made red and green tinsel into a wreath which she wore as a crown.

'How are we doing for time?' she asked.

Tamsin looked at her watch. 'About ten minutes.' she paused, 'do you remember in August after that wedding when you first told me of your idea?'

'The night we designed the flyers – well you designed the flyers.'

'And you said, build it and they will come. Well they came, nearly a hundred of them. And they're still here. Even Moira with the broken wrist has made it after all. You have a choir and they're all part of it.'

'Well we'd better get them singing then.' Jenny had had enough emotional sentimentality for one day.

'Right, I'll go and get them on to the stage, and once they're on and I'm at the piano, you come in and weave your magic.'.

Jenny was left alone. She ran through the first bars of the first couple of pieces in her head. She could hear applause, that would be the choir getting into position. She opened the door slightly and peeped through. All she could see were the dancers sitting at the far side. Then the lights on them also went down and there was an expectant hush in the darkness. She hoped there would be enough light for her to grope her way to her music stand.

The choir had done an amazing job of selling tickets. The church congregation were there, together with Pauline's Baptists. Mercifully not in kit, Molly Button morris dancers had turned up in strength along with some of Stefan's Royal Mail colleagues. Many of the Polish dominoes club were there. Mr Braithwaite had come for the first half. Then there were individual friends and relatives of the choir members. Tim was pleased to see James, what he assumed were his parents and a young lady who could have been either a sister or a girlfriend. He really must talk to James more. He was relieved to see that the frightening Ms Stephenson didn't appear among those present.

Dr Trev had arrived half an hour before the performance and met up with Amanda. His fiancee had arrived ten minutes earlier and was sitting in the nave where she had struck up a conversation with a woman who was a professional actor in a touring theatre group and had come to support her friend from the same group who was in the choir. They excused themselves and joined the rest of the choir in the reserved seating.

A substantial cohort of Kimz Kidz families had managed to lay claim to many of the front seats and appeared to have brought as many children to sit in the audience as they had to take part in the performance. With five minutes to go before the start, the latest arrivals were having to stand at the back whilst Colin, aided by Ben and his crew passed spare chairs from various small rooms off the nave. Eventually everyone was seated.

John, June and Sophie handed over the box office to Frances and joined the choir as they walked onto the platform. The lights slowly went down and an expectant silence spread like a blanket over the audience.

At 7.31 Jenny stepped through the doors and walked towards her music stand. The back row of the choir started to applaud and this was taken up by the audience. She couldn't see very well in the dark but she could feel the presence of the huge audience. She stepped onto the little platform prepared for her, bowed and turned to the choir, shrouded as they were in darkness. She hoped Ben knew what he was doing with the lights and they would be able to see each other – as well as the audience seeing them. This was it, guys, the first performance. A spotlight picked her out, isolating her from the darkness. She smiled and raised her hands and the choir stood up. She nodded to where she knew Tamsin and the piano was and was rewarded with a G major chord. A second spot light picked out Tim. There was silence. A long expectant silence. Oh God he'd dried or forgotten the words. But then he opened his mouth and recreated the performance from the afternoon. If anything, it was better.

As the lights gradually came up she could finally see the choir clearly. They had taken her at her word. In the darkness she had thought Tiny Tim was wearing an evening suit but now she could see it was a knitted tail suit and bow tie with some kind of sparkle entwined. It was a fraction too small which added to the comic effect. Next to him Nigel had a Christmas jumper with a long thin plum pudding on it and June Ferguson's made her look like a rather elderly fairy.

Mr Crowther had a knitted Santa Top to which he'd added a knitted yellow mayor's chain of office. Every member of her choir had obviously gone all out to enter into the spirit of the evening. The Indian lady had a Christmas tree jumper which Jenny was to discover before the end of the evening lit up with fifty little bulbs. Even Colette had a jumper with a reindeer on it, thanks to Mrs Winston's credit card.

Tim's solo reached its end and he was rewarded by tumultuous applause.

Phoebe stepped forward and announced the Cowboy Carol which the youngsters in the audience clearly enjoyed and this was followed by Silent Night.

Then it was the turn of the youngest of Kim'z Kidz. Ben from the lights had been persuaded to double as sound engineer and as the tots pirouetted and hopped through their routines there were 'Oos' and 'Aws' from the audience, and not just from the parents of those taking part.

And then it was back to the choir. And then more dancing. And the choir again.

And before anyone realised it they had reached 'Gaudete' and it was time for the interval.

Jenny sat in the Lady Chapel, collecting her wits. OK, so there had been odd bits of faulty intonation and not all the dynamics she'd rehearsed had been remembered but these were not professional singers. These were newsagents and librarians and widowed teachers who in a dozen rehearsals had produced this. She thought of the first time she had come with Colin into this depressing old echoing building. And now it was filled with people and light and music. She thought of all the people who had had faith in her dream, Mr Braithwaite, Mr Crowther and The Vicar of Doom. And the transformation of the Valentines and June Ferguson and Tiny Tim, dear big loveable Tim.

And then it was time for the second half.

They started with Away in a Manger which the dance school joined in singing with. Then it was All I want for Christmas is My Two Front Teeth which mercifully they had decided to do without actions, although Jenny caught sight of Colette twitching to have a go. Then Kimz Kidz did a dance interpretation of the nativity story. By now Jenny had relaxed enough to enjoy it. Then she was back up directing the choir. They swung through De Virgin Mary and the rest of their programme, shared again with items by the dance school. And then, all too soon, it was O Come All Ye Faithful with the audience joining in and the choir providing the soaring descant.

And then it was over.

There was clapping and stamping and even some whistles.

Jenny bowed. She acknowledged the choir. She acknowledged Tamsin. She bowed again. What a pity there hadn't been time to record the occasion. Still, she felt most of the choir would have happy memories of the night.

Sophie, selected as the youngest member of the choir, brought on a small bouquet for Tamsin and another for Jenny. One of the tiny dancers brought on one as big as herself for Kim.

Colin stood up and thanked everybody, performers, technicians, ticket sellers and finally the audience. He explained that the profits from the concert were going to the Samaritans who were so busy at Christmas time. He emphasised how many people were lonely with no one to share Christmas with.

Barbara looked out at the audience. She could see Howie and Debbie sitting on each side of her ex, Ken. As he was still on his own she thought she might invite him over for Christmas dinner. The fact that the kids would like that was her justification.

Mr Rossini in the tenors caught Mrs Winston's eye in the sopranos and winked. She stifled a giggle. She didn't think either of them would be lonely this Christmas. She looked around the audience and suddenly saw Mrs Milner, Colette's mum. She'd actually made the effort to come to see her daughter sing. Or, as Colette would say, she'd bothered. Wonders would never cease.

Her daughter, Colette, meanwhile had spotted Tom Clancy about five rows back who immediately gave her a thumbs up and a cheeky grin. He probably would have been less happy if he'd realised that sitting next to him was Sergeant Oldham from the local police, fulfilling his promise to Susie Blake to come to her first concert.

Tim was so proud. Old Mr Thicket had made it. He was sitting halfway back with a very attractive lady, one he recognised from the photos at Mr Thicket's house as Charlie, Mr Thicket's daughter. The photos didn't do her justice. He thought about the name of the company, his company – Jolley and Son. It really should be Dalby. Or Dalby and Son. Well it would never be Dalby and Son unless he took steps to make something happen.

After all, if he could stand up in church and do a solo, he could surely ask a gorgeous looking woman to go out for a drink.

Sophie saw her mum and Tony sneaking out at the back. She was glad she'd written and invited her and pleased she'd come.

Suddenly, out of the blue, Jenny spotted a middle-aged couple. How had she missed them at the interval. But there they were. All the way from Wakefield. She could hardly wait for Colin to finish so she could ask how they'd got there and if they were staying somewhere overnight.

Colin was drawing to a close saying something about loved ones at Christmas. He urged them to give generously and turned to Jenny. He thanked her for putting the whole thing together and then he stopped. There was an awkward pause. She realised she was expected to say or do something and she had nothing ready. She knew she should have prepared an encore but there hadn't been time. And then, not for the first time, a huge figure came to her rescue. Without warning Tiny Tim stood up and started 'On the first day of Christmas my true love sent to me.' With the actions. He stood on one leg with his arms out.. 'A partridge in a pear tree'. The audience laughed. For verse two the choir joined in and by the twelfth day, everybody was standing and singing and performing the actions, even the Vicar of Doom.

And later a lot of happy people left the church and crossed the road to the Crown.

Chapter 46 : Jenny's review

The first thing Jenny noticed in the crowded bar was that Sam and Carl had been joined by Mr Braithwaite who had his jacket off, his sleeves rolled up and was pulling pints as though he'd done it all his life. Which, of course, for much of it he had. Kim had obviously disposed of Kimz Kidz back to parents because she was now helping out. Jenny hadn't yet been made aware that Kim was going to take over from Carl now he was in charge of the IT at Nigel's chambers. In fact Mr Braithwaite had spoken to Sam about becoming area manager to see if he could breathe life into some of the other pubs and they were even considering making Kim the licensee after some training. Although on Saturdays and Sundays she would need to arrange cover downstairs whilst Kimz Kidz trained upstairs. And Thursday was choir night!

Tiny Tim was in his element surrounded by a number of the sopranos and altos although he was talking mainly to a very attractive woman Jenny didn't recognise.

The two doctors were talking to a beautiful, sophisticated woman who was introduced to Jenny as Dr Trev's sister, Cerys. After a split second Jenny was able to place her as the woman she had noticed talking to Dr Trev in the pub in the lake district. Apparently she was a director of a clothing business in Manchester and owned some property in the area including the pub.

Pauline and Sheena were going the rounds with a twig of mistletoe.

Tim was hoping they wouldn't come near him, whilst Charlie

thought it might be fun if they did. Her father had told her about Tim the artist and she knew he had taken over Jolley's and was making a huge success of it. She had seen a cutting about his famous overpowering of the mugger and tonight she had seen him in action. And she liked what she saw. If he didn't offer to buy her a drink in a minute she would have to make the first move. Fortunately that didn't become necessary. After a couple of false starts Tim not only bought her a drink but also arranged that she would meet him the following day after the switching on of the lights and go for dinner. Tim wasn't sure whether he should try out the Bentley for the first time now he had it taxed and insured. He decided against it. It would be a bit showy.

Susie Blake was chatting to Nigel as usual and June Ferguson was in one corner helping Sophie's dad count the charity money.

There was the middle-aged Welshman she recognised as Mr Thomas from the school speaking to Mrs Valentino. They seemed to be discussing Mrs Valentino going back to teaching English part-time. She wondered what would happen to Mr Carlston. He wouldn't go to prison, not just for possession - assuming it was his first offence - but she doubted he would be allowed back to Brunswick High. From the little she knew and had heard, that was possibly a good thing for all concerned. She wondered if he would come back to the choir. She was relieved she had decided not to set up the school choir. Another girl, Helen had taken on that mantle. Jenny hoped she would get on OK.

Sam had brought the keyboard downstairs and Pauline's brother, Leroy, was playing Christmas music. Some of the choir were singing along. He had a jazzy style with some interesting harmonies and Jenny decided to make an effort to talk to him later. Not because he was incredibly handsome with an infectious smile but because of his musicianship she told herself.

Eventually she found her parents. She was beginning to wonder if they'd gone straight back to Yorkshire but they were happily chatting to Tamsin and Stuart. It turned out they had booked into a nearby hotel and asked Jenny what her plans were for the next day or was she free to come to the hotel for lunch. Jenny actually had a number of things scheduled for the next day, all of which she instantly decided to postpone. Mum and dad could stay until the early evening so had time to come to the switching on of the Christmas lights before catching their train.

In the far corner Leroy now had a group singing Rudolph the Red-nosed Reindeer.

Sophie came up to say thank you. When Jenny said, ' That's not necessary. I love running the choir and making this music,' Sophie said ' Not just making the music, but making people happy and well again. Look at my dad and Miss Ferguson. She's coming to have Christmas dinner with us. The choir made that happen.

'I didn't realise,' said Jenny.

'And, miss, I know I would have to learn to read music and everything but, well one day I wish I could make a choir like this. If dad and June and me keep coming to choir, do you think I could learn how.'

'I'm sure you could.' She smiled at the young teenager.

Leroy had moved on to Chestnuts Roasting on an Open Fire.

It was Tamsin's turn. 'She's right. It is about a lot more than the music, Jenny. Look at Tim, how he's blossomed.'

'Yes, who's that girl he's with?'

'Ah, turns out it's the daughter of his old art master, the one that started him off carving. I think we need to recruit her to the choir quickly before she recruits him away from it. With all his strengths, I've never thought of Tim as romantic but tonight I've seen him in a new light. And look at Mr and Mrs Valentino – who aren't really married or called that. But give it time. And Kimz Kidz. And Colette.'

Jenny was beginning to feel embarrassed but was spared further compliments when the Vicar of Doom arrived with Frances. He was another who looked happier than she had ever seen him and she introduced Frances to Tamsin.

'Yes, we met earlier,' said Tamsin, 'because I hadn't realised Colin was married'.

'Ah, the power behind the throne,' said Jenny who was still in the middle of realising it and noticing they both wore wedding rings.'

'Well that was very worthwhile,' Colin said, oblivious to Jenny's discomfort. 'I am so glad you are supporting the Samaritans. What made you choose them?'

'You did,' smiled Jenny, relieved to change the conversation. 'That first time you brought me to St Peter's we talked about neighbours and strangers and you asked me to read Luke chapter 10 verse 28. I did.'

'Ah, the story of the good Samaritan. Well, thank you,' said Colin. 'The gospel of St Mark chapter 4 verse 3 onwards would seem to be appropriate.'

Jenny stored this at the back of her mind to look up later but said, 'While you're here, Tamsin arranged a little collection among the choir for the church – to pay for the heating and lighting that we used. And to thank you.' And in the time honoured tradition of musicians everywhere, she passed him an envelope.

Colin started to say it was nothing but Jenny carried on, ' No, not for the use of the building, well not just that, but for your faith in us. You said,'Build it and they will come'. And they did, didn't they?'

Colin thought for a moment, 'There are different kinds of faith,' was all he said.

Leroy was improvising around Mistletoe and Wine as Ben and his team arrived. Jenny saw him pass car keys to Tim and give a thumbs up sign. Did that mean the lights were already down and in the back of Tim's van. It certainly looked like it. This seemed to be confirmed when Colin went out presumably to lock the church.

Pauline and Sheena had reached the Valentinos and held the mistletoe over their heads. There was a pause that felt like eternity to both of them. Then Valerie turned her head and kissed Valentino on the lips. It was not a kiss full of passion or lust, but one much more of gentle tenderness and affection. And as they drew apart, Nigel joked 'Jut wait till Valentine's Day', which made everyone laugh. Although that was the point when Mrs Winston decided she had no intention of waiting till Valentine's Day. She was nearly 53. She'd spent too much of her recent time waiting. Tonight when Mr Rossini walked her home she would invite him in for coffee as she always did, but this time to include breakfast.

A lady Jenny didn't recognise touched Jenny's arm and introduced herself as Bea, Ben's partner. She said how much she'd enjoyed the show and said she hoped Jenny wouldn't mind but she had videoed the whole show. Would Jenny like a copy. Before Jenny finished thanking her and saying they would be in touch to see about selling copies to the choir Tamsin drew Jenny to one side.

'Jenny, I need to have a word.'

'What's the problem?'

'In the new year I'm afraid I'm only going to be able to play for you until Easter.'

'Why – what's wrong?'

'Nothing's wrong, but by June I might not be able to reach the keyboard.'

'Why ever not? Tamsin, what are you talking about?'

'Jenny, I've been to see Amanda at the doctors. I'm pregnant'.

As if triggered by mental telepathy, Leroy switched to When a Child is Born.

Jenny stood stunned then grabbed her friend and hugged her. 'Tamsin, I am so pleased for you both.

So when's it due?'

'Not till late July but I wanted you to have plenty of warning.'

Jenny did the maths. 'October, in the lake district. That day you got lost?'

Tamsin blushed slightly. 'Possibly.'

'I don't know how we'll replace you but that's my problem. Is it still a secret?'

'I suspect it won't be for much longer. I told Stuart this afternoon and look at him now. Whatever he says, he'll blurt it out to someone before the end of the evening. And as for a replacement, why not go and chat to Pauline's brother, Leroy, before he escapes tonight. He certainly sounds competent and he is, how can I put this, very decorative.'

Jenny turned and looked at him. He certainly was decorative – very decorative. And he had a nice, light, jazzy piano style. Jenny had already made up her mind to go and speak to him before they closed the night's proceedings. She noticed Colin and Ben returning and Bill Crowther getting Ben and his team drinks.

Then it was June Ferguson's turn. 'Could we have a little hush please'

'Good Lord, she thinks she's back in the library,' said a voice which might have been Nigel's. There were giggles.

'John and I have counted the ticket money and the bucket collection at the end and the Samaritans will be receiving a cheque for eight..'

'...pounds fifty.' The witty voice was traced to Nigel.

June was not to be put off, 'Eight hundred and seventy four pounds, thirty seven pence.'

Jenny was speechless. How much?

Suddenly Tim was on his feet. 'Three cheers for miss Jenny,' he cried, hip hip, hooray; hip, hip, hooray; hip, hip, hooray.'

Jenny felt she ought to respond so started, 'Ladies and gentlemen,'

The choir all joined in with, 'Much as we are enjoying ourselves there are a few business matters to sort out.'

Jenny struggled to keep a straight face, 'Next term's programme will include Mozart's Ave Verum, A selection of Abba's greatest hits, A section of the Petite Messe Solennelle by the other, more famous, Mr Rossini and 4 songs from Porgy and Bess.

Don't forget tomorrow, 4 o'clock by the Christmas tree, as many as can, for the switching on of the lights. Merrry Christmas to all of you'.

And as she passed Tamsin a white envelope, fuller than either of them had expected when they had started out on this adventure, it was left to Tiny Tim to have the final word as with a huge smile he said, ' God Bless Us, Everyone.'